CORN + GUACAMOLE + LIME + CILANTRO + TORTILLA CHIPS

CHICKEN BURRITO BOWL

GRILLED CHICKEN + QUINOA + LETTUCE + CHEESE

PAGE 115

BUILD-A-BOWL

WHOLE GRAIN + VEGETABLE + PROTEIN + SAUCE = MEAL

NICKI SIZEMORE

Storey Publishing

The mission of Storey Publishing is to serve our customers by publishing practical information that encourages personal independence in harmony with the environment.

Edited by Deanna F. Cook and Lisa H. Hiley
Art direction and book design by Jeff Stiefel
Text production by Slavica A. Walzl
Indexed by Christine R. Lindemer, Boston Road Communications
Cover and interior photography by © Katrin Björk, except
© Alessandro de Leo/Alamy Stock Photo, 81;
© Ira Heuvelman - Dobrolyubova/Getty Images, 162;
© Jeremy Iwanga/Unsplash, 24; Mars Vilaubi, 50 right, 51;
© WiktorD/iStockphoto.com, 50 left
Food styling by Tehra Thorp
Illustrations by © Georgina Luck

Storey Publishing
210 MASS MoCA Way
North Adams, MA 01247
storey.com

Printed in China by Toppan Leefung Printing Ltd.
10 9 8 7 6 5 4 3 2 1

Library of Congress Cataloging-in-Publication Data

Names: Sizemore, Nicki, author.
Title: Build-a-bowl / Nicki Sizemore.
Description: North Adams, MA : Storey Publishing, [2018] | Includes index.
Identifiers: LCCN 2018012682 (print) | LCCN 2018024000 (ebook)
ISBN 9781612129914 (ebook) | ISBN 9781612129907 (pbk. : alk. paper)
Subjects: LCSH: One-dish meals. | LCGFT: Cookbooks.
Classification: LCC TX840.O53 (ebook) | LCC TX840.O53 S59 2018 (print)
DDC 641.82—dc23
LC record available at https://lccn.loc.gov/2018012682

FOR
JAMES

CONTENTS

INTRODUCTION

I don't know about you, but for me the dinnertime scramble is real. Whether you have a job or kids or both, it can be a struggle to satisfy the desire to eat something vibrant and delectable without having hours to spend in the kitchen. After my second daughter was born, I had less time than ever, but I didn't want to give up on my commitment to feeding my family well. Oh, all right; that's a lie. In truth, I didn't want to give up my desire to eat good food every night.

My mission is to help you make homemade, healthy, *freaking delicious* meals any day of the week, and this is the easiest way I know how. Here's the lowdown:

Grains + Vegetables + Protein + Sauce + Garnish = Superpower Meal

I'm no mathematician, but that formula might just win you the Nobel Peace Prize (at least from your family). Each recipe in this book is a complete, balanced meal, meaning there's no deciding what to pair with the entrée or scrambling to make side dishes. With plenty of options for customization, the recipes appeal to different palates and lifestyles. Perhaps best of all, every meal comes together in less than an hour if you have a batch of precooked grains at the ready (more on that later).

THE WORLD IS NOW AT OUR FINGERTIPS WITH REGARD TO FOOD SELECTION, WITH A WIDER AVAILABILITY OF PRODUCE, HERBS, SPICES, NUTS, AND GRAINS THAN EVER BEFORE. THE RECIPES IN THESE PAGES DRAW ON INFLUENCES FROM CULTURES NEAR AND FAR.

I'm a texture and flavor fanatic. As a trained cook, I spend my days developing an array of recipes for articles, clients, and my website, From Scratch Fast, but my hands-down favorite way to eat is to throw a bunch of different ingredients into one bowl over a bed of grains, then drizzle everything with a quick sauce. The contrast of warm, cool, crunchy, soft, salty, and sweet is pure magic — it's simple home cooking at its most exciting. And yet, at the same time, it's pure comfort. One-bowl meals have nourished cultures around the world for centuries, from European breakfast porridges to Korean rice bowls to Andean quinoa stews. Grain bowls are in our DNA.

But we've come a long way since the time of our ancestors. The world is now at our fingertips with regard to food selection, with a wider availability of produce, herbs, spices, nuts, and grains than ever before. The recipes in these pages draw on influences from cultures near and far — from Mexico to Thailand to the Middle East to Italy to Korea to my own backyard garden — using easy-to-find supermarket ingredients. Vegetable fried "rice" (page 75) is topped with creamy avocado slices and toasted cashews; Moroccan-spiced lamb patties (page 146) are accompanied by garlicky zucchini and a coconut-spiked mint and cilantro sauce; and crispy fish taco bowls (page 154) are brightened up with a quick cabbage slaw and a creamy chipotle sauce.

For finicky eaters (ahem, such as my two girls, Ella and Juniper), several of the recipes can be broken down into individual components to pick and choose from, burrito bar–style. So while 3-year-old Juni inhales the black beans in the roasted cauliflower and squash bowls (page 106), 8-year-old Ella prefers to load up on the cauliflower instead (although she still has to try the beans — the rule in our house is that you have to try everything, even if you don't eat much). My spice-loving husband, James, can liberally douse his bibimbap-style steak bowl (page 137) with gochujang sauce, while I go for a bigger serving of sesame carrots and kimchi.

And while James and I prefer to layer everything together in one bowl for the ultimate expression of flavors and textures, Ella and Juniper insist that they'll die if their broccoli touches their meatballs. With the exception of the fruity breakfast bowls and the soup and salad recipes, their meals are served in little bundles on plates, with the sauce on the side for dipping. That's okay, too.

About that sauce: The easiest way to transform an ordinary meal into something spectacular is to drizzle it with a creamy, garlicky, herby, or spicy sauce. But let me assure you that sauces don't have to be complicated or timely affairs. The sauces in this book — from a smoky red pepper sauce (page 61) to an herbed yogurt sauce (page 157) to a pea pesto (page 63) to an herby vinaigrette (page 169) — come together in minutes, can often be made well in advance, and usually don't require the stove. Some recipes don't even need a sauce at all; in those cases, a drizzle of hot sauce or a spritz of citrus juice does the trick. While I've paired the sauces with specific dishes, you can also mix and match them in a choose-your-own-adventure style of eating.

Now back to those grains. Whole grains are my secret weapon for throwing together quick and healthy weeknight meals. Not only are they inexpensive and highly nutritious, but their mild flavor is also perfect for soaking up sauces, vinaigrettes, and dressings. Perhaps most important, they can be made weeks or even months ahead of time, as can many other components of these recipes (woot woot!). With a batch of cooked grains waiting for me in the refrigerator or freezer, dinner feels like it's already started, even if I haven't done a thing. According to my calculations, that means I'm 76 percent more likely to make dinner on exhausted evenings than resort to take-out pizza.

In these pages, you'll find everything from rice to quinoa to millet to Khorasan wheat (Kamut) and more. Most of the grains are considered ancient grains, which are superfoods that are rich in vitamins, minerals, and protein. Luckily for us, they are all now widely available and easy to cook. I encourage you to step out of your comfort zone and try something new!

I hope you enjoy this book, and I would *love* to hear from you! Please feel free to share your questions and comments (and photos!). And, as always, happy cooking!

Nicki

The Build-a-Bowl MEAL FORMULA

GRAINS + VEGETABLES + PROTEIN + SAUCE + GARNISH = SUPERPOWER MEAL!

Choose your grains: start with about ½ cup of grains (make the grains in big batches ahead of time for quicker meals).

Add two or more vegetables: combine different textures and colors, both cooked and raw, using seasonal produce when possible. Or use fruit!

Pick a protein: opt for a lean protein, such as beans, eggs, poultry, grass-fed beef, lamb, fish, seafood, tofu, or cheese.

Drizzle with a sauce: a vibrant sauce or a drizzle of hot sauce or citrus juice ties everything together and takes the bowl from ordinary to extraordinary.

Finish crunchy and bright: a smattering of something crispy (such as nuts or seeds) provides a pop of texture, while fresh herbs brighten up flavors.

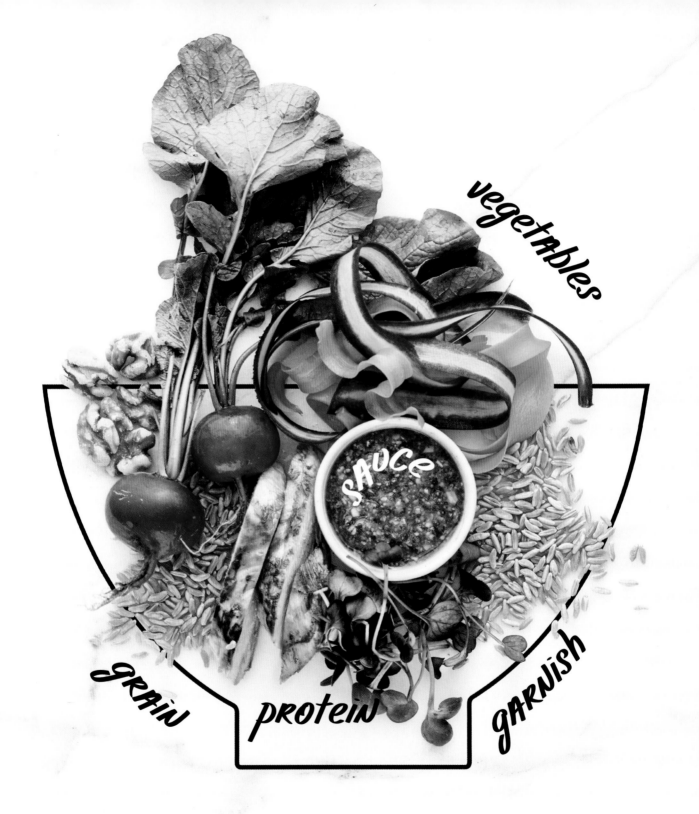

BUILD-A-BOWL BASICS

My goal is to help you whip up exciting, nourishing meals, from breakfast all the way to dinner. I've included fruity breakfast porridges, egg bowls, salads, hearty vegetarian dishes, lean meat mains, and more. These are some of my family's very favorite meals, and I hope they'll become some of yours, too. Following are a few of my tips for getting good food on your plate (or rather, in your bowl) even on a hectic Wednesday. And remember, every cook and kitchen is different, so I encourage you to follow your own instincts as you go!

NUTS AND SEEDS

A sprinkle of toasted nuts and seeds is an easy way to add an instant pop of texture and flavor to your bowls. Since many of the recipes in this book include seeds and nuts in some form, I suggest either buying them pretoasted (if available) or toasting up big batches ahead of time. That way, they'll be ready and waiting for you. Store toasted nuts and seeds in sealed containers in the refrigerator or freezer to keep them fresh.

For cashews, almonds, walnuts, hazelnuts, and pecans: Spread the nuts in an even layer on a large baking sheet, and bake them in a 350°F (180°C) oven for 5 to 10 minutes, until fragrant and slightly darkened. Keep your eye on them during the last few minutes of cooking (and use a timer — I've burned more batches of nuts than I care to admit). For hazelnuts, rub the toasted nuts in a clean kitchen towel to remove the skins.

For pine nuts, pepitas, sunflower seeds, hemp seeds, and sesame seeds: Spread the nuts or seeds in a large skillet (I prefer to use the stovetop instead of the oven, as they go from golden to blackened quickly) and place it over medium heat. Cook, stirring often, until the nuts are golden and fragrant (the pepitas will also puff up), 4 to 6 minutes.

DIETARY RESTRICTIONS? (NO PROBLEM!)

If you don't eat gluten, don't worry. Every single recipe in this book is gluten-free as long as you use one of the gluten-free grains (the grains are all tagged). If you don't eat meat, there are a slew of plant-based dishes as well as numerous variations for vegetarians. And if you don't eat grains at all, most of the recipes are just as delicious without them!

MAKE-AHEAD OPTIONS

For me, this is key. If you're able to leisurely cook breakfast and dinner every night, then you can skip this section. (And may I please come over? I'll do the dishes!) But if breakfast and dinner are usually rushed affairs, then read on.

While these recipes are simple, they're made of a few moving parts (that's what makes them interesting). So while you can absolutely start each recipe from scratch, if you can manage to knock out one or two tasks before the mealtime hour rolls around, then it's going to give you a big leg up. From cooking a few batches of grains days or even weeks in advance (see page 6) to making a couple of sauces on the weekend to roasting a batch of vegetables the night before to buzzing up a dressing before work, completing even the smallest of tasks ahead of time can have a big payoff later.

I find that the mental relief of having a few things ready might be even more important than the actual time saved. It's one less thing to think about while I simultaneously steam the green beans, unpack bags, help with homework, manage a meltdown, and post pictures to Instagram (priorities, people).

USE WHAT YOU HAVE

Do you have half of a bell pepper in the fridge that needs to get eaten? Slice it up and toss it in with the sautéed vegetables! Do you have a bunch of kale that's hiding in the back of your vegetable drawer? Swap it in for the spinach! Not a meat eater? Slide on an egg instead of the roasted shrimp! No grains in the pantry? Serve the meal on pasta instead!

You get it.

I encourage you to make these recipes your own, using items you have on hand or can easily find. I try to include variations where I can in the recipe notes, and I urge you to customize these recipes according to your own tastes and lifestyle.

SEASON AS YOU GO

I don't include salt and pepper quantities in my recipes unless a specific amount is necessary (such as for the grains, but you can cut back on the salt if you prefer) because seasoning is highly subjective. Not only that, the kosher salt I buy (Diamond Crystal, if you're interested) might be a totally different weight and salinity than the salt you use, meaning my teaspoon of salt could be way less salty than yours. So go ahead and season to your own tastes!

That being said, after teaching cooking classes for more than a decade, I've found that most people actually don't use enough salt, which can leave a dish or a sauce tasting flat. So unless you need to limit sodium for health reasons, be generous with your seasoning. Taste as you go, and season throughout the cooking process.

BOWLS . . . OR PLATES

All of the recipes are designed as one-dish, complete meals, with layers of flavors that complement one another. Shallow bowls work great for this style of eating, but, with the exception of the breakfast porridges and soups, you can most certainly use plates, tire hubs, Frisbees, or whatever you usually eat off of. Also, you can either build your bowls in the kitchen before serving or you can serve each of the components separately on the table and let your friends or family build their own. If you're feeding kids, this gives them the freedom to choose what they want while also expanding their palates. I'll never forget the day Ella went back for seconds of the roasted broccoli after vowing for years that she hated it. It was better than Christmas.

ABOUT GRAINS

As a key source of complex carbohydrates and protein, grains have been at the root of human evolution since we discovered agriculture about 10,000 years ago. In this book, I feature both true grains and pseudo-cereal grains (a term that for some reason makes me think of Clark Kent). By definition, grains are cultivated cereals — the small, dry seeds that come from grasses, including wheat, barley, oats, millet, and rice. Pseudo-cereals (in their brown suits with thick black glasses), including quinoa and buckwheat, are not actually members of the grass family, so aren't technically grains. But since I'm a firm believer in non-discrimination, I'm just going to refer to everything as grains.

Most of the varieties included in these pages, including quinoa, millet, sorghum, buckwheat, spelt, Khorasan wheat (Kamut), farro, einkorn, and barley, are considered ancient grains, meaning they are largely untouched by selective breeding and have hardly changed in the past several millennia. These ancient grains are often higher in fiber, protein, vitamins, and minerals than hybrids, and some people find that they're easier to digest. Quinoa, millet, sorghum, and buckwheat are also all gluten-free, as are the rice varieties.

WHAT ABOUT GRAIN-FREE DIETS?

Let's talk about the elephant in the room: what about the recent rise in popularity of grain-free diets such as the paleo diet? While whole grains have a long history of providing essential nutrients to humans and have an important place on my table, if a grain-free diet works for you, then go for it. In fact, with the exception of the breakfast bowls, the majority of recipes in this book can be made without the grains or with a grain-free substitute, such as cauliflower rice.

GAS VS. ELECTRIC

Boiling grains is no biggie no matter what stove you have, but there's one slight change if you own an electric stove. When making quick-cooking grains such as rice, quinoa, millet, or buckwheat, instead of simply turning the heat to low once the water comes to a boil, slide the pot over to another burner that's preheated to low. The reason for this is that it can take a few minutes for the electric coils to cool from high to low heat (unlike a gas flame, which changes immediately). Those few minutes can mean the difference between mushy rice and perfectly cooked rice, hence the switch!

NUTRITIONAL POWERHOUSES

Whole, unprocessed grains are extremely nutritious. They're high in fiber, protein, B vitamins, iron, and magnesium. And as complex carbohydrates, they trigger the release of serotonin, our "happy hormone," without resulting in a sugar crash. Studies also indicate that whole grains can help guard against obesity and can even help with healthy sleep patterns. Best of all, they're inexpensive and easy to make and they store wonderfully. Unlike pasta or potatoes, you can cook them well in advance — we're talking days, weeks, or even months ahead of time! — so that they're ready and waiting for you when the mealtime rush begins.

TIPS FOR COOKING GRAINS

Let's say it together: "Cook ahead!" This is the single most important thing that I will tell you in this chapter. If you have a premade batch of grains ready and waiting for you in the fridge or freezer, then you're only a few steps away from an awesome meal. In fact, all of the bowl recipes in this book come together in less than an hour (some far less), with the assumption that your grains are precooked.

The second most important tip is, make a big batch. If you can, carve out some time on the weekend, in the morning before work, or at night while you're watching Netflix to cook your grains (the only grain that I don't usually make ahead is white rice, as the texture is best straight from the pot). Cooked grains can happily chill in the refrigerator for up to five days or in the freezer for up to three months. Sundays are usually my big-batch day, when I whip up one or two grains for the week, often making double batches of each so that I can freeze half for meals down the line (boom!).

But let's be real. There are evenings when I haven't planned ahead and the freezer stash has run dry. No fear! Cooking grains is mostly a hands-off affair, and they can simmer away while you prep the rest of dinner. Quinoa, millet, white rice, and buckwheat are the quickest cooking of the bunch and are my go-tos for those "$#%&-it's-six-o'clock-and-I-haven't-started-dinner-yet" nights.

STORING AND REHEATING

If you make your grains in advance (you're amazing!), transfer them to a wide bowl or a large baking sheet and let them cool completely. Store them in a sealed container if they're going in the fridge. For freezing, I prefer to use labeled quart-size ziplock freezer bags. That way they can be stacked in a tidy pile without taking up too much space. Defrost the grains in the refrigerator overnight, at room temperature for a few hours (you can immerse the bag in warm water to expedite the process), or in the microwave (transfer the grains to a bowl and microwave them on medium power in 1-minute intervals, stirring between each, until thawed).

For salads, sautés, and stir-fries, you can use the grains cold, straight out of the fridge. For other recipes, reheat the grains in the microwave for 1 to 3 minutes, until warmed through. Or reheat them on the stovetop in a nonstick skillet or in a pot with a splash of oil, butter, or water; cook, stirring occasionally, until warm.

RICE COOKER VS. STOVETOP

I offer two foolproof methods for cooking your grains: on the stovetop or in a rice cooker. There are merits and minuses to both.

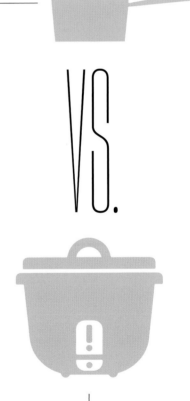

RICE COOKER

The benefit of using the rice cooker is that you can set it and forget it. If you need to run out and pick up the kids (or have a tipple with friends), you can leave your rice cooker to do its thing. A lot of new models can also be programmed ahead, meaning you can set it a few hours in advance.

The downside is that grains often take longer to cook in the rice cooker, and you lose control over the cooking process. I find that, with the exception of rice, grains often end up slightly overcooked or even occasionally undercooked, especially ones that need to be soaked first and that only work in models with a brown rice setting. However, I *always* use my rice cooker when making rice, because I suffer from post-traumatic stress disorder from years of overcooking rice on the stove.

STOVETOP

The stovetop is the most accurate way to cook grains, as you have more control over the cooking process. This is especially true for hearty varieties, such as wheat and barley, which can vary pretty widely in their cooking times depending on the age of the grains, the brand, the specific variety, and so on. When you use the stovetop, it's easy to check for doneness by tasting occasionally.

The drawback is that you have to be at least minimally present. You don't need to be at the stovetop or even in the kitchen for most of the time, but you'll need to monitor the grains toward the end, so no jetting off to the local watering hole.

MEASURE . . . OR NOT

You know how sometimes you just can't be bothered with digging out the measuring cups (or is that just me)? I have good news. While each grain recipe lists specific grain-to-water ratios, I hereby give you permission to disregard them. Well, sort of. Instead of measuring water, you can prepare the grains "pasta-style," whereby you cook them in a large pot of simmering water, just as you would pasta. This works best for larger, chewier grains, such as sorghum, any of the wheat varieties, and barley. Bring a large pot of water to a boil, and season it with salt. Add the grains, cook at a gentle boil until they reach your desired tenderness, then drain.

No matter which cooking style you use, the best tool in your kitchen to test whether the grains are done is your teeth! Different batches of even the same grain can cook differently depending on their age and brand, so use the times in this book as guidelines. Let your mouth be the final test.

WATER OR BROTH

All of the recipes call for cooking the grains in water, giving them a neutral, clean flavor that's really versatile. However, you can swap in broth or stock for a more robust flavor when making savory dishes. You can also add aromatics to the cooking liquid, such as whole spices (cinnamon sticks, cloves, bay leaves, allspice), garlic cloves, halved shallots, citrus peel, or parsley sprigs. Just be sure that the flavors pair well with the other elements in the final dish (so no garlic in that fruity breakfast bowl, please!).

SOAK OR NO SOAK

You have the option to soak your grains before cooking. This means simply covering the grains with water and letting them sit at room temperature for several hours or overnight. While this is optional (except when cooking certain hearty grains in the rice cooker), there are some fantastic benefits to soaking your grains.

MORE NUTRITIOUS. All whole grains contain phytic acid, an antinutrient that blocks the absorption of vitamins and minerals in your body. Soaking helps to remove this acid, rendering the grains more nutritious and easier to digest. Adding a splash of lemon juice or vinegar to the soaking water will neutralize this acid even further.

BETTER TEXTURE. Soaking results in a more consistent, even texture. This is especially true for buckwheat, sorghum, wheat varieties, brown rice, and black rice.

SHORTER COOKING TIME. You can shave off up to 15 minutes of the cooking time by soaking your grains first.

However, if you don't have the time or forget to soak your grains, or if you choose not to, no worries! You can absolutely still charge ahead with cooking them — just rinse them in cold water first to remove any dust or impurities on the surface.

BUYING & STORING

One of the best sources for buying grains is your local farmers' market. Purchasing from local farmers ensures not only that you're getting the freshest product possible but also that you're supporting the environment and your local community.

Most grocery stores also now carry a wide variety of grains, sold either in bulk bins or with the packaged goods. The bulk bins are often the cheapest way to go, but you have no way of knowing how old the grains are. Whole grains are susceptible to rancidity, so try to buy from stores that have a heavy turnover. Also, give the grains a whiff before buying — they should smell fresh and nutty (if they smell funky or unpleasant, they have likely gone off). Similarly, if you buy grains in packages, be sure to check their expiration dates. Bob's Red Mill is a reliable, easy-to-find brand.

Once you get home, store the grains in airtight containers (if they're not already in one) or in ziplock bags. It's best to store them in the freezer or refrigerator if you have the space, but if not, buy smaller quantities and keep them at room temperature. I store most of my grains in jars in my pantry, as we use them up quickly.

COOKING
GRAINS

Cooking grains is as elemental as it gets, involving nothing more than water and salt. The process couldn't be easier: once the grains are rinsed or soaked, the stovetop or rice cooker does most of the work for you. Use the cooking times on the following pages as guidelines — the best way to check for doneness is by tasting.

I strongly suggest doubling these recipes and freezing half for breakfasts and dinners down the line — your future self will thank you! Also, be sure to read my make-ahead and storage tips in the preceding chapter.

While each of these grains has its own unique character in terms of flavor and texture, they are interchangeable in the superpower meal recipes except for where a particular grain is specified. I hope you'll explore each of them and discover new favorites!

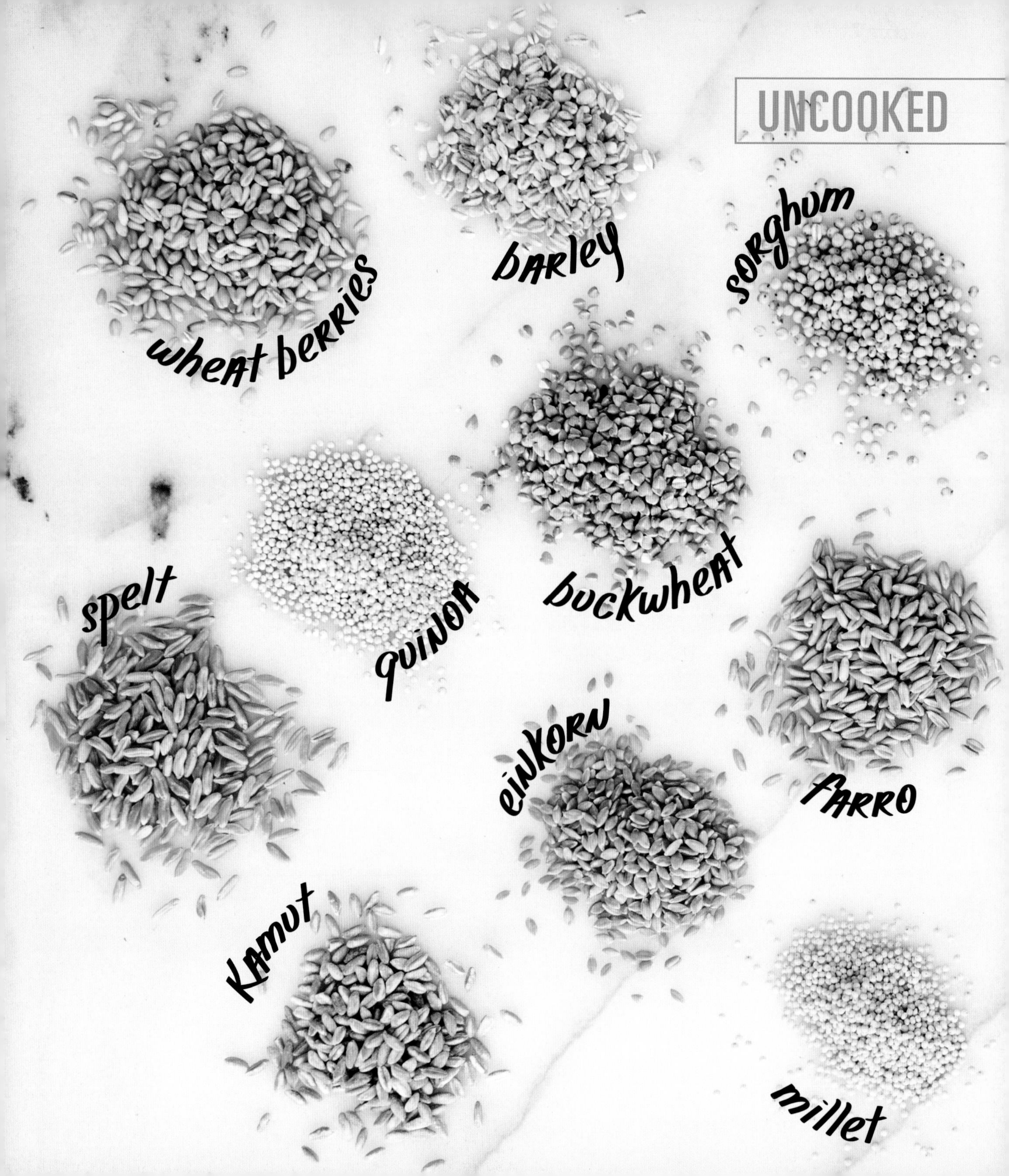

UNCOOKED

wheat berries

barley

sorghum

spelt

quinoa

buckwheat

farro

einkorn

kamut

millet

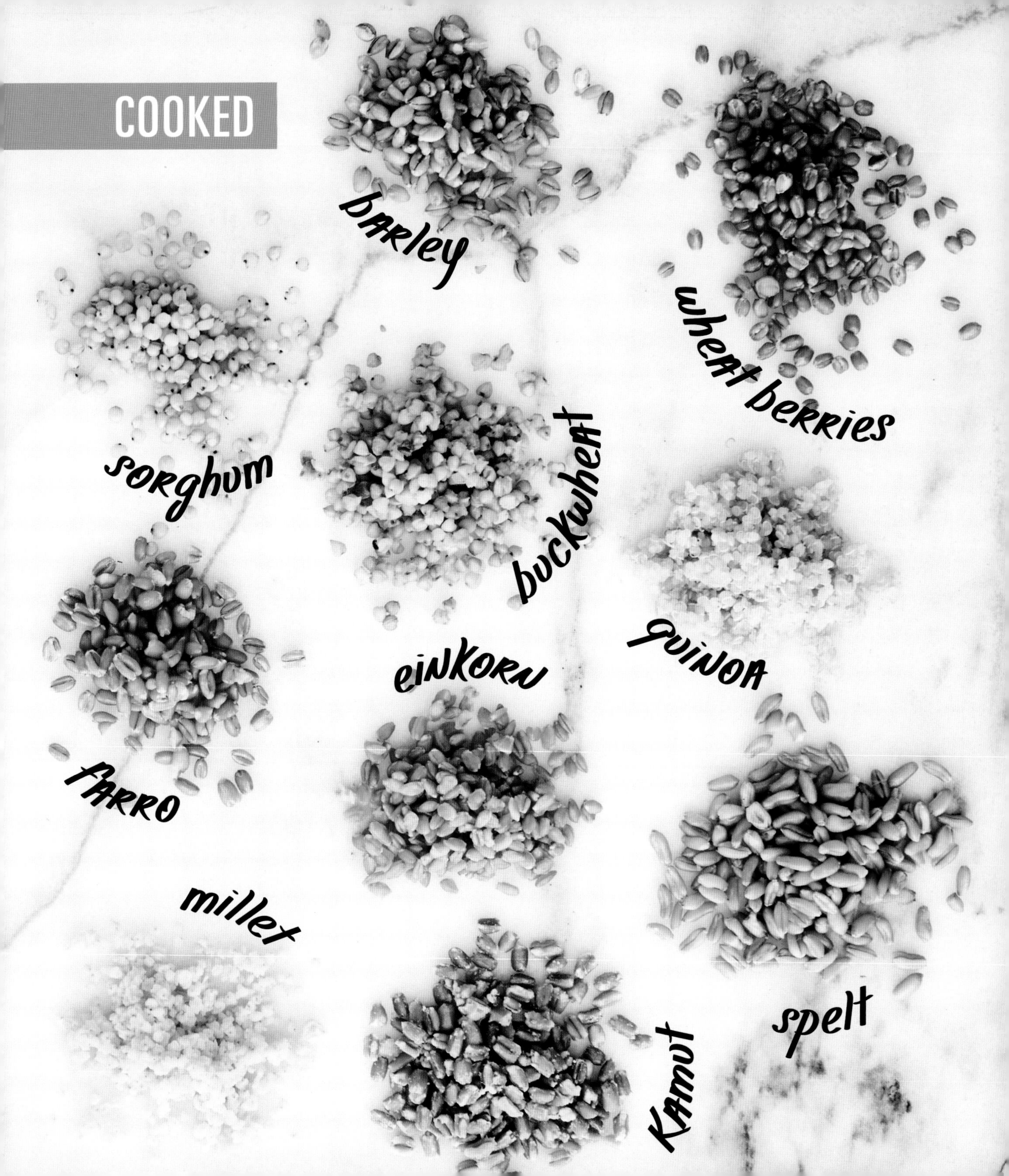

barley

wheat berries

sorghum

buckwheat

quinoa

einkorn

farro

millet

kamut

spelt

amaranth

wild rice

oat groats

rye berries

freekeh

teff

OTHER GRAINS TO EXPLORE

This book includes some of the most versatile and common whole grains, but there are still more! Check out these other tasty grains.

RYE BERRIES AND TRITICALE. Much like wheat or barley, rye berries have a hearty, chewy texture, but they have a more distinctive flavor (think rye bread). Triticale is a hybrid of wheat and rye.

BULGUR AND FREEKEH. Made from cracked dried wheat, bulgur and freekeh are both quick-cooking grains that work well in salads and pilafs. Bulgur is mild (it's the grain traditionally used in tabbouleh), while freekeh has a slightly smoky flavor.

OAT GROATS. Before they're flattened, rolled oats start as oat groats, which look similar to wheat berries. They're chewy and robust, with an oat-y flavor.

AMARANTH. This gluten-free seed is a complete protein. It has an earthy, nutty flavor and, when cooked, a thick, porridgelike texture that works best in breakfast bowls.

TEFF. The smallest grain in the world, teff is naturally gluten-free. Like amaranth, it has a unique flavor and porridgelike texture that works well in breakfast bowls.

WILD RICE. With its distinct nutty flavor, wild rice — which is actually a grass, not a rice — is delicious in pilafs and salads and as a bed for hearty toppings.

BARLEY

FLAVOR: NUTTY / TEXTURE: CHEWY

Barley is the fourth most cultivated grain in the world, behind corn, rice, and wheat. Like wheat, it's a member of the grass family, with a history that stretches back 10,000 years. Barley grains have a slightly more robust nutty and sweet flavor than wheat berries, lending themselves well to salads, soups, and stews (and brewing . . . think beer!).

Hulled barley is considered a whole grain, unlike its pearled brethren, and it is very high in fiber. It's also a lower-glycemic food, meaning it doesn't cause spikes in blood sugar. When shopping, look for hulled or hull-less barley as opposed to pearl barley, which has been polished to remove the bran and often the germ, where most of the nutrition resides.

IF SOAKING: Place the grains in a medium bowl and cover with 2 to 3 inches of warm water. Let sit at room temperature for 10 to 12 hours (or overnight). Drain and rinse. Reduce the cooking water to 2¼ cups. Reduce the cooking time to 30 to 35 minutes if cooking on the stovetop.

STOVETOP

Rinse the barley in cold water, and drain well. Place the grains in a medium pot and add the water and salt. Bring to a boil, then reduce the heat to a simmer. Cover and cook until the grains are tender yet chewy, 40 to 50 minutes. Remove the pot from the heat and let sit for 5 minutes to steam. Drain off any excess water.

RICE COOKER

Soak the barley as directed above. Place the grains, 2¼ cups of water, and the salt in the rice cooker. Cover and cook using the brown rice setting. Fluff the barley with a fork before serving.

1 cup hulled or hull-less barley (not pearled)

2½ cups water

½ teaspoon kosher salt

MAKES: ABOUT 2½ CUPS

COOKING TIME

30-35 MINUTES SOAKED

40-50 MINUTES UNSOAKED

PLUS 5 MINUTES TO STEAM

1 cup raw buckwheat groats (not toasted buckwheat or kasha)

2 cups water

½ teaspoon kosher salt

MAKES: ABOUT 2½ CUPS

COOKING TIME

4–5 MINUTES SOAKED

10–12 MINUTES UNSOAKED

KASHA

You might be familiar with toasted buckwheat groats, called kasha, which are commonly cooked with milk or water and served as porridge in Eastern European cultures. While it's delicious on its own, I find that kasha is too strongly flavored for grain bowls, where it tends to compete with the other ingredients. Stick to the milder untoasted groats.

BUCKWHEAT

FLAVOR: EARTHY, NUTTY / TEXTURE: SOFT, SOMETIMES PORRIDGELIKE / GLUTEN-FREE

Contrary to its name, buckwheat has no relation to wheat — in fact, it's a gluten-free seed! Buckwheat is thought to have been first cultivated in Southeast Asia around 8,000 years ago, from where it then spread to the Middle East and Europe. It's now a dietary staple in Russia and Eastern Europe.

I've found that different brands vary quite widely in the way they cook, with some turning rather mushy. I've had the most luck with European imported varieties as opposed to what's usually found in bulk bins. That being said, I don't always mind it having a porridgelike texture, particularly in cold-weather breakfast bowls (such as the Triple-Chocolate Buckwheat bowls on page 46) or as a bed for rich meats or sauces. It's supremely comforting, particularly when finished with a knob or two of butter.

Soaking before cooking creates a better texture, but if it soaks for too long the grains will break down. Four hours seems to be the sweet spot, and from there it only takes five minutes to cook.

IF SOAKING: Place the grains in a medium bowl and cover with 2 to 3 inches of warm water. Let sit at room temperature for 4 hours. Drain and rinse well (the grains will become quite slimy). Reduce the cooking water to ½ cup. Reduce the cooking time to 4 to 5 minutes. Stir once or twice during the cooking time.

STOVETOP

Rinse the buckwheat in cold water, and drain well. Place the grains in a medium pot and add the water and salt. Bring to a boil, then reduce the heat to a simmer (if using an electric stove, slide the pot to another burner preheated to low). Cover and cook until the grains are tender and the water has been absorbed, 10 to 12 minutes.

RICE COOKER

I don't recommend cooking buckwheat in a rice cooker, as it will get too mushy.

MILLET

FLAVOR: MILD, CORNLIKE / TEXTURE: FLUFFY / GLUTEN-FREE

Millet is a versatile and quick-cooking grain with a nutty, cornlike flavor. Its origins extend back to ancient times, when it was farmed by the Egyptians, Greeks, and Romans and revered as a sacred crop in China. Today you'll find hulled millet at most grocery stores. It can be cooked into a fluffy side dish (much like polenta), into a creamy base for meats or vegetables, or into a comforting breakfast porridge (check out the Millet Muesli bowls on page 37).

Millet is high in fiber and provides important vitamins and minerals, such as phosphorus, magnesium, and vitamin B_6. It's also naturally gluten-free and is one of the only alkaline grains, meaning it's easily digestible and doesn't create acidity in the body.

Because millet is so small, 1 cup produces a relatively large quantity of cooked grains compared to the other grains in this book. You might not need to use a full batch in the bowl recipes, so reserve any leftovers for breakfast or lunch the next day!

1 cup millet
2 cups water
½ teaspoon kosher salt

MAKES: ABOUT 3½ CUPS

COOKING TIME
12 MINUTES SOAKED
15 MINUTES UNSOAKED
PLUS 10 MINUTES TO STEAM

IF SOAKING: Place the grains in a medium bowl and cover with 2 to 3 inches of warm water. Let sit at room temperature for 10 to 12 hours (or overnight). Drain and rinse. Reduce the cooking water to 1½ cups. Reduce the cooking time to 12 minutes if cooking on the stovetop.

STOVETOP

Rinse the millet in cold water, and drain well. Bring the water to a boil in a medium pot. Add the millet and the salt. Bring the water back to a boil, then reduce the heat to a simmer (if using an electric stove, slide the pot to another burner preheated to low). Cover and cook until all of the water has been absorbed (you should see little divots in the millet), about 15 minutes. Remove the pot from the heat and let sit, covered, for 10 minutes to steam. Fluff the millet with a fork before serving.

RICE COOKER

Rinse the millet in cold water, and drain well. Place the grains, water, and salt in the rice cooker. Cover and cook using the white rice setting. Fluff the millet with a fork before serving.

MAKE IT CREAMY

For a less fluffy and creamier, porridgelike consistency, increase the amount of water to 3 cups, and cook as instructed.

QUINOA

FLAVOR: GRASSY / TEXTURE: FLUFFY / GLUTEN-FREE

Once almost unknown in the United States, quinoa is now a commonplace grain across the country. It originated with the Incas in the Andes Mountains, where it's still a prominent food source, and it's one of the only ancient grains that contains all nine essential amino acids, making it a complete protein.

Quinoa is high in fiber and a good source of antioxidants and minerals. It's also one of the few alkaline grains, meaning it doesn't create acidity in the body. There are more than 100 varieties of quinoa (!!), but white, red, and black quinoa are the most common (red and black varieties have a slightly stronger flavor, but they're also higher in antioxidants). With its fluffy texture, quinoa is perfect for grain bowls or in pilafs, stews, or breakfast porridges.

Quinoa is small, so 1 cup produces a relatively large quantity of cooked grains compared to the others in this book. You might not need to use a full batch in the bowl recipes, so reserve any leftovers for future meals.

IF SOAKING: Place the grains in a medium bowl and cover with 2 to 3 inches of warm water. Let sit at room temperature for 10 to 12 hours (or overnight). Drain and rinse. Reduce the cooking water to 1½ cups. Reduce the cooking time to 12 to 15 minutes if cooking on the stovetop.

STOVETOP

Rinse the quinoa in cold water, and drain well. Place the grains in a medium pot and add the water and salt. Bring to a boil, then reduce the heat to a simmer (if using an electric stove, slide the pot to another burner preheated to low). Cover and cook until the grains have started to unfurl and all of the water has been absorbed (you should see little divots in the quinoa), 15 to 17 minutes. Remove the pot from the heat and let sit, covered, for 10 minutes to steam. Fluff the quinoa with a fork before serving.

RICE COOKER

Rinse the quinoa in cold water, and drain well. Place the grains, water, and salt in the rice cooker. Cover and cook using the white rice setting. Fluff the quinoa with a fork before serving.

1 cup quinoa (white, red, or black)

2 cups water

½ teaspoon kosher salt

MAKES: ABOUT 3½ CUPS

COOKING TIME

12–15 MINUTES SOAKED

15–17 MINUTES UNSOAKED

PLUS 10 MINUTES TO STEAM

RICE VARIETIES

Rice is one of the most widely consumed staple foods for a large part of the world's population, especially in Asia. It has a long and important history, feeding more people over a longer stretch of time than any other crop. There are thought to be more than 40,000 varieties of cultivated rice, but for the sake of sanity (mine and yours), I'm sticking with white, brown, and black rice, which are all widely available.

ARSENIC IN RICE

During the past few years, arsenic in rice has become a concern, as it can accumulate in the grains from pesticides and fertilizers found in soils and groundwater. There are a few things you can do to reduce your exposure to arsenic in rice. First, seek out organic rice grown in California or rice from the Himalayan region; they appear to have lower levels of arsenic than rice grown in other regions. Second, wash the rice well in several changes of fresh water. Finally, eat rice in moderation as part of a varied diet, and limit your consumption of rice-based products, such as rice milk, crackers, and cereals. For more information, visit consumerreports.org.

BLACK RICE

FLAVOR: NUTTY, SWEET / TEXTURE: STICKY, CHEWY / GLUTEN-FREE

Sometimes referred to as "forbidden rice" or "emperor's rice" because it was once reserved for Chinese royalty, black rice is an heirloom variety of rice that has been enjoyed in Asia for thousands of years. Luckily for us, it's now available in grocery stores and specialty markets across the United States.

Black rice is possibly the most nutritious of all rice varieties. Like brown rice, it has its bran layer and germ intact, but black rice also has one of the highest concentrations of anthocyanins (the highly beneficial antioxidants that are responsible for the deep blue, red, and magenta pigments in blueberries, eggplant, and grapes) in food, which are linked to a decreased risk for heart disease and cancer. It's also high in fiber, iron, and vitamin E.

Black rice has a nutty, slightly sweet flavor and chewy, pleasantly sticky texture.

IF SOAKING: Place the grains in a medium bowl and cover with 2 to 3 inches of warm water. Let sit at room temperature for 10 to 12 hours (or overnight). Drain and rinse. Reduce the amount of cooking water to 1¾ cups. Reduce the cooking time to 25 to 30 minutes if using the stovetop.

STOVETOP

Rinse the rice in a strainer under cold running water, swishing the grains with your fingers, until the water runs clear. Drain well. Bring the water to a boil in a medium pot and add the rice and salt. Return the mixture to a boil, then reduce the heat to a simmer (if using an electric stove, slide the pot to another burner preheated to low). Cover and cook until all of the water has been absorbed, 35 to 40 minutes. Remove the pot from the heat and let sit, covered, for 10 minutes to steam. Fluff the rice with a fork before serving.

RICE COOKER

Rinse the rice in a strainer under cold running water, swishing the grains with your fingers, until the water runs clear. Drain well. Transfer the rice to the rice cooker, and add the water and salt. Cover and cook using the brown rice setting. Fluff the rice with a fork before serving.

1 cup black rice
2 cups water
½ teaspoon kosher salt

MAKES: ABOUT 3 CUPS

COOKING TIME
25-30 MINUTES SOAKED
35-40 MINUTES UNSOAKED
PLUS 10 MINUTES TO STEAM

BROWN RICE

FLAVOR: NUTTY, FRAGRANT / TEXTURE: CHEWY, FLUFFY / GLUTEN-FREE

A poster child of the healthy food revolution, brown rice has become a staple on grocery store shelves and in kitchens over the past few decades. Unlike white rice, which is milled and refined, brown rice is a whole grain, containing the outer bran layer and germ, which is where most of the vitamins and nutrients reside. It's high in fiber and is a good source of magnesium, iron, and B vitamins.

I prefer to soak brown rice before cooking, which results in a fluffier, more evenly cooked texture as well as a faster cooking time. Soaking may also help to lower levels of arsenic in brown rice, which are generally higher than in white rice because arsenic accumulates in the grain's outer layers. Seek out long-grain brown rice varieties, preferably organic, from California, India, or Pakistan, which appear to have less arsenic than brown rice from other regions.

IF SOAKING: Place the grains in a medium bowl and cover with 2 to 3 inches of warm water. Let sit at room temperature for 10 to 12 hours (or overnight). Drain and rinse. Reduce the amount of cooking water to 1½ cups. Reduce the cooking time to 30 to 35 minutes if cooking on the stovetop.

STOVETOP

Rinse the rice in a strainer under cold running water, swishing the grains with your fingers, until the water runs clear. Drain well. Bring the water to a boil in a medium pot and add the rice and salt. Return the mixture to a boil, then reduce the heat to a simmer (if using an electric stove, slide the pot to another burner preheated to low). Cover and cook until all of the water has been absorbed, 35 to 45 minutes. Remove the pot from the heat and let sit, covered, for 10 minutes to steam. Fluff the rice with a fork before serving.

RICE COOKER

Rinse the rice in a strainer under cold running water, swishing the grains with your fingers, until the water runs clear. Drain well. Transfer the rice to the slow cooker, and add the water and salt. Cover and cook using the brown rice setting. Fluff the rice with a fork before serving.

1 cup brown rice

1¾ cups water

½ teaspoon kosher salt

MAKES: ABOUT 3 CUPS

COOKING TIME

30-35 MINUTES SOAKED

35-45 MINUTES UNSOAKED

PLUS 10 MINUTES TO STEAM

WHITE RICE

FLAVOR: MILD TO FRAGRANT / TEXTURE: FLUFFY / GLUTEN-FREE

White rice is the only grain in this book that's not a true "whole grain," since the bran and germ are removed. While this process also removes most of the grain's nutritional value, I'd argue that there's still a place for white rice on our tables — nothing can beat its neutral, slightly sweet flavor as a counterpart to highly seasoned sauces or delicate fish (think of it as the little black dress of cooking — you might not wear it often, but it's easily accessorized and oh-so-adaptable).

When shopping for white rice, steer clear of enriched varieties, which usually cook up flavorless and mushy. Instead, opt for long-grain basmati or jasmine varieties, which are fluffy and fragrant. Swishing the rice in several batches of cold water before cooking removes the starches on the surface, preventing the rice from turning gummy.

Soaking is not recommended.

STOVETOP

Bring the water to a boil in a medium pot. Place the rice in a bowl and cover with cold water. Swish the rice with your fingers, then drain off the water. Repeat the process until the water runs clear. Drain well. Transfer the rice to the boiling water and add the salt. Return the water to a boil, then reduce the heat to a simmer (if using an electric stove, slide the pot to another burner preheated to low). Cover and cook until all of the water has been absorbed (you should see little divots in the rice), 15 to 17 minutes. Remove the pot from the heat and let sit, covered, for 10 minutes to steam. Fluff the rice with a fork before serving.

RICE COOKER

Place the rice in a bowl and cover with cold water. Swish the rice with your fingers, then drain off the water. Repeat the process until the water runs clear. Drain well, then transfer the rice to the rice cooker. Add the water and salt. Cover and cook using the white rice setting. Fluff the rice with a fork before serving.

1½ cups water

1 cup medium- or long-grain white rice

½ teaspoon kosher salt

MAKES: ABOUT 3 CUPS

COOKING TIME
15–17 MINUTES
PLUS 10 MINUTES TO STEAM

SORGHUM

FLAVOR: MILD / TEXTURE: CHEWY / GLUTEN-FREE

Sorghum is probably one of the least familiar of all the grains in this book, but it's one of the most versatile. It has a chewy texture like wheat berries but with a milder flavor, and it's naturally gluten-free. Sorghum originated in Africa and spread to other semiarid areas, where it remains a principal food grain, used primarily to make beer, porridge, and flour. It's rich in iron and protein and is a good source of minerals, fiber, and antioxidants. In addition, the slow-digesting starches make it a good choice for diabetics. The cooked grains can be eaten warm, at room temperature, or cold in salads. Some varieties can even be popped like popcorn in a hot skillet!

IF SOAKING: Place the grains in a medium bowl and cover with 2 inches of warm water. Let sit at room temperature for 8 to 12 hours (or overnight). Drain and rinse. Reduce the cooking water to 2½ cups. Reduce the cooking time to 35 to 45 minutes if cooking on the stovetop.

STOVETOP

Rinse the sorghum in cold water, and drain well. Place the grains in a medium pot and add the water and salt. Bring to a boil, then reduce the heat to a simmer. Cover and cook until the grains are tender but still chewy, 50 to 60 minutes (if the grains are still crunchy, add another cup of water and continue simmering). Drain off any excess water. Fluff the sorghum with a fork before serving.

RICE COOKER

Rinse the sorghum in cold water, and drain well. Place the grains, water, and salt in the rice cooker. Cover and cook using the brown rice setting. Drain off any excess water. Fluff the sorghum with a fork before serving.

1 cup sorghum

3 cups water

½ teaspoon kosher salt

MAKES: ABOUT 2½ CUPS

COOKING TIME

35-45 MINUTES SOAKED

50-60 MINUTES UNSOAKED

WHEAT VARIETIES

Although we're most familiar with wheat in its milled form as flour, unprocessed wheat kernels are a good source of vitamins, minerals, fiber, and protein. The whole grains retain their bran and germ, which is where most of the nutrition resides. While you can find standard wheat berries in nearly any grocery store, ancient and heirloom wheat varieties, such as einkorn, spelt, Khorasan wheat (Kamut), and farro, are all becoming increasingly available and offer more in terms of flavor and nutrition. All of these grains are fantastic in bowls, side dishes, and salads.

EINKORN

FLAVOR: NUTTY / TEXTURE: CHEWY

Einkorn was one of the first plants cultivated by humans about 10,000 years ago with the birth of agriculture in the Fertile Crescent. While production was abundant in ancient times in regions such as the South Caucasus, Middle East, southwestern Europe, and the Mediterranean, the grain nearly went extinct during the past few millennia, replaced by modern wheat varieties, which are easier to grow and have higher yields. Luckily for us, growers in parts of the United States and Italy are currently investing in its production, largely due to its nutritional profile — einkorn has a higher protein content than commercial wheat and is lower in gluten, making it more easily digestible for many people. It's also a good source of B vitamins.

IF SOAKING: Place the einkorn in a medium bowl and cover with 2 to 3 inches of warm water. Let sit at room temperature for 10 to 12 hours (or overnight). Drain and rinse. Reduce the cooking water to 2 cups. Reduce the cooking time to 20 to 25 minutes if cooking on the stovetop.

STOVETOP

Rinse the einkorn berries in cold water, and drain well. Place the grains in a medium pot and add the water and salt. Bring to a boil, then reduce the heat to a simmer. Cover and cook until the grains are tender but still chewy, 30 to 35 minutes. Remove the pot from the heat and let sit, covered, for 5 minutes to steam. Drain off any excess water. Fluff the einkorn with a fork before serving.

RICE COOKER

Rinse the einkorn berries in cold water, and drain well. Place the grains, water, and salt in the rice cooker. Cook on the brown rice setting. Fluff the einkorn with a fork before serving.

1 cup einkorn wheat berries
2½ cups water
½ teaspoon kosher salt

MAKES: ABOUT 2 CUPS

COOKING TIME
20–25 MINUTES SOAKED
30–35 MINUTES UNSOAKED
PLUS 5 MINUTES TO STEAM

GET TOASTY

Intensify the nutty flavor of whole grains by toasting them before cooking. Spread the grains on a baking sheet and bake in a 375°F (190°C) oven for 5 to 10 minutes, until fragrant and lightly browned.

FARRO

FLAVOR: NUTTY / TEXTURE: CHEWY

Farro, or more specifically, *farro medio*, is the Italian name for emmer wheat, an ancient grain with a nutty flavor and chewy texture (you might also see *farro piccolo* and *farro grande*, which refer to einkorn and spelt, respectively). A staple in the diets of ancient Romans, farro is having a comeback, appearing across the United States on restaurant menus and in home kitchens as a side dish, in salads, or even as a substitute for rice in risotto.

I prefer to use whole-grain farro, which has the highest concentration of nutrients and fiber, as opposed to pearl or semipearl, which have had part of the bran removed. Farro is high in fiber and is a good source of iron and protein.

IF SOAKING: Place the grains in a medium bowl and cover with 2 to 3 inches of warm water. Let sit at room temperature for 10 to 12 hours (or overnight). Drain and rinse. Reduce the cooking water to 2 cups. Reduce the cooking time to 10 to 12 minutes if cooking on the stovetop.

STOVETOP

Rinse the farro in cold water, and drain well. Place the grains in a medium pot and add the water and salt. Bring to a boil, then reduce the heat to a simmer. Cover and cook until the grains are tender but still chewy, 25 to 35 minutes. Remove the pot from the heat and let sit, covered, for 5 minutes to steam. Drain off any excess water. Fluff the farro with a fork before serving.

RICE COOKER

Rinse the farro in cold water, and drain well. Place the farro, water, and salt in the rice cooker. Cover and cook using the brown rice setting. Fluff the farro with a fork before serving.

1 cup whole-grain farro (not pearled)

2½ cups water

½ teaspoon kosher salt

MAKES: ABOUT 2 CUPS

COOKING TIME

10-12 MINUTES SOAKED

25-35 MINUTES UNSOAKED

PLUS 5 MINUTES TO STEAM

KHORASAN WHEAT (KAMUT)

FLAVOR: MILD, NUTTY / TEXTURE: CHEWY

Also known as Kamut, Khorasan wheat is an ancient grain that most likely originated in the Fertile Crescent. It was allegedly found in Egyptian tombs, giving it the nickname "King Tut's wheat." The grain reached the United States in the middle of the twentieth century and was trademarked in the late 1970s by farmers in Montana.

Kamut must be organic and can never be hybridized or genetically modified. It looks similar to wheat berries, but with a longer shape. It also has a higher protein content than most modern wheat and is a good source of fiber, amino acids, vitamins, and minerals.

IF SOAKING: Place the Khorasan wheat in a medium bowl and cover with 2 to 3 inches of warm water. Let sit at room temperature for 10 to 12 hours (or overnight). Drain and rinse. Reduce the cooking water to 2 cups. Reduce the cooking time to 30 to 45 minutes if cooking on the stovetop.

STOVETOP

Rinse the Khorasan wheat in cold water, and drain well. Place the grains in a medium pot and add the water and salt. Bring to a boil, then reduce the heat to a simmer. Cover and cook until the grains are tender but still chewy, 45 to 60 minutes. Remove the pot from the heat and let sit, covered, for 5 minutes to steam. Drain off any excess water. Fluff with a fork before serving.

RICE COOKER

Soak the Khorasan wheat as directed above. Drain and rinse. Place the grains, 2 cups of water, and the salt in the rice cooker. Cover and cook using the brown rice setting. Fluff with a fork before serving.

1 cup Khorasan wheat (Kamut)
2½ cups water
½ teaspoon kosher salt

MAKES: ABOUT 2 CUPS

COOKING TIME
30–45 MINUTES SOAKED
45–60 MINUTES UNSOAKED
PLUS 5 MINUTES TO STEAM

SPELT BERRIES

FLAVOR: NUTTY / TEXTURE: CHEWY

Spelt is an older cousin to modern durum wheat. It originated about 8,000 years ago in the Near East and then spread to Europe, where it was an important staple during the Middle Ages. It was introduced to America in the late nineteenth century and has recently resurged in popularity as a wheat substitute in artisanal and commercial baked goods, breads, and cereals. Some people find spelt easier to digest than modern wheat. It's a good source of fiber, protein, iron, and manganese.

IF SOAKING: Place the spelt berries in a medium bowl and cover with 2 to 3 inches of warm water. Let sit at room temperature for 10 to 12 hours (or overnight). Drain and rinse. Reduce the cooking water to 2 cups. Reduce the cooking time to 35 to 45 minutes if cooking on the stovetop.

STOVETOP

Rinse the spelt berries in cold water, and drain well. Place the grains in a medium pot and add the water and salt. Bring to a boil, then reduce the heat to a simmer. Cover and cook until the grains are tender but still chewy, 45 to 55 minutes. Remove the pot from the heat and let sit, covered, for 5 minutes to steam. Drain off any excess water. Fluff the spelt berries with a fork before serving.

RICE COOKER

Soak the spelt berries as directed above. Drain and rinse. Place the grains, 2¼ cups of water, and the salt in the rice cooker. Cook on the brown rice setting. If the berries are still slightly crunchy after the machine beeps, close the lid and let steam for 10 to 20 minutes. Fluff the spelt berries with a fork before serving.

1 cup spelt berries

2½ cups water

½ teaspoon kosher salt

MAKES: ABOUT 2 CUPS

COOKING TIME

35–45 MINUTES SOAKED

45–55 MINUTES UNSOAKED

PLUS 5 MINUTES TO STEAM

WHEAT BERRIES

FLAVOR: NUTTY / TEXTURE: CHEWY

Most of the whole-wheat flours and baked goods we find in the market are milled from wheat berries, which typically come from modern, hybrid strains of wheat. There are different varieties of wheat berries named according to their growing season (spring vs. winter), gluten content (hard vs. soft), and color (red vs. white). White wheat is slightly milder in flavor than red wheat, while hard wheat is higher in gluten and protein (making it ideal for bread baking, while soft wheat is often used in pastries).

    The cooking process is the same for all the berries, but hard wheat varieties usually take a bit longer to become tender. Wheat berries are high in fiber, protein, and B vitamins.

IF SOAKING: Place the wheat berries in a medium bowl and cover with 2 to 3 inches of warm water. Let sit at room temperature for 10 to 12 hours (or overnight). Drain and rinse. Reduce the cooking water to 2 cups. Reduce the cooking time to 35 to 45 minutes if cooking on the stovetop.

STOVETOP

Rinse the wheat berries in cold water, and drain well. Place the grains in a medium pot and add the water and salt. Bring to a boil, then reduce the heat to a simmer. Cover and cook until the grains are tender but still chewy, 45 to 55 minutes. Remove the pot from the heat and let sit, covered, for 5 minutes to steam. Drain off any excess water. Fluff the wheat berries with a fork before serving.

RICE COOKER

Soak the wheat berries as directed above. Drain and rinse. Place the grains, 2¼ cups of water, and the salt in the rice cooker. Cook on the brown rice setting. If the berries are still slightly crunchy after the machine beeps, close the lid and let steam for 10 to 20 minutes. Fluff the wheat berries with a fork before serving.

1 cup wheat berries
2½ cups water
½ teaspoon kosher salt

MAKES: ABOUT 2 CUPS

COOKING TIME
35–45 MINUTES SOAKED
45–55 MINUTES UNSOAKED
PLUS 5 MINUTES TO STEAM

Build-a-Bowl

MEALS

It's time to strap on your cape — or apron, that is! Don't worry, you won't need any superpowers to whip up these meals. The dishes on the following pages are packed with flavor and nutrition, with an approachable spin that makes them easy enough to master in any home kitchen. They can all be made in less than an hour, assuming that you have a batch of cooked grains on hand (be sure to check out chapter 2 for tips on cooking, storing, and reheating grains). If you haven't precooked the grains, simply start them first, and let them do their thing while you get moving on the rest of the recipe. Many recipes also offer make-ahead options for other ingredients — look for those tips.

There are a slew of plant-based options, as well as several vegetarian variations in the meat and fish chapters. Every single recipe is also naturally gluten-free, as long as you use a gluten-free grain. As far as the meat and fish chapters go, I think it's important to be mindful of the products we buy. Pasture-raised, grass-fed, and/or organic meats, as well as wild, sustainably caught fish, are often better for our bodies and the environment. Most of the recipes feature a bit less protein than you would typically buy to feed four people since the dishes are packed with grains and vegetables, so go for high-quality meat if you can.

All right, friends, let's get cooking!

MILLET MUESLI, PAGE 37

FRUIT

No matter how prepared we are or how early we wake up, mornings are a hustle. Between dragging the kids out of bed, getting ourselves ready, and making our way downstairs (often counting every. single. step. in slow motion with our 3-year-old), breakfasts have to be efficient. But I'm a stickler when it comes to the morning meal. While cereal is fine on occasion, I truly believe that starting the day with something warm and nourishing, filled with protein, fiber, and healthy fats, makes a big difference in the outcome of the day, improving moods and giving us enough brainpower to get to lunch. Plus, if we fill up on good stuff at breakfast, I'm less worried about what we eat (or what the kids don't eat) the rest of the day.

These beautiful fruity breakfast bowls (which can be eaten anytime and are also some of our favorite snacks) come together quickly, especially if you make the toppings in advance, such as caramelized apples that taste just like pie, roasted rhubarb and strawberries that you will want to eat with a spoon, fresh peaches with cashew cream, and citrus segments with coconut. Warm up a batch of grains in some milk or nut milk, spoon on the toppings, sprinkle with chopped nuts or granola for crunch, and you're on your way to a very good day indeed.

BANANA BREAD BOWL

3 medium ripe bananas

1 tablespoon unsalted butter or virgin coconut oil, plus more for serving

1 tablespoon packed brown sugar

1 batch cooked brown rice

1 tablespoon ground flaxseeds

Milk (unsweetened nut, coconut, soy, or regular milk), as needed

Coarsely chopped toasted walnuts or pecans, for serving

Flaky sea salt, for serving

If a hug had a flavor, this is what it would taste like. These bowls transform banana bread into a quick, soul-satisfying breakfast that's far healthier than your grandma's sugar- and fat-laden loaf recipe but still oh-so-good. I prefer to use brown rice in these bowls, because it lets the banana flavor shine.

The rice is sweetened with a touch of brown sugar and a mashed banana, cooked until lightly caramelized for added complexity. Finish the bowl off with a knob of butter, sliced bananas, toasted nuts, and a pinch of sea salt (trust me on this), and let it wrap its warm arms around you.

SERVES 4 | PREP TIME: 5 minutes | COOKING TIME: 10 minutes

1 Using a fork, mash one of the bananas into a purée.

2 Melt the butter in a medium pot over medium heat. Add the sugar and cook, stirring with a rubber spatula, for 1 minute. Scrape in the banana purée and cook, stirring, for 1 to 2 minutes (things should be smelling quite good at this point!). Slide in the rice and flaxseeds, and stir to combine. Pour in enough milk to loosen the mixture. Bring to a simmer and cook for 5 minutes.

3 Slice the remaining 2 bananas.

4 Spoon the warm grains into bowls. Top each bowl with a knob of butter, sliced bananas, toasted walnuts, and a sprinkle of sea salt.

APPLE CRISP BOWL

Once the mornings start to turn colder, I need all the help I can get to motivate my kids out of bed. Luckily I have these nutritious breakfast bowls in my arsenal, which I think you will love, too. The smell alone is enough to draw slippered feet down the stairs.

With cinnamon-scented caramelized apples, warm buttery grains, maple syrup, and crunchy granola or roasted nuts, they have all the flavors of an apple crisp. The caramelized apples are also delicious over ice cream, mixed into yogurt, or on pancakes.

SERVES 4 | PREP TIME: 5 minutes | COOKING TIME: 10 minutes

1 Place the grains in a medium pot and add enough milk to loosen them. Bring to a simmer. Stir in a knob or two of butter. Keep warm over low heat.

MAKE THE APPLES

2 Melt the 2 tablespoons of butter in a large skillet over medium heat. Add the apples and season with a small pinch of salt; toss to coat. Cook, stirring occasionally, until the apples are lightly browned and tender, 5 to 7 minutes. Add the cinnamon, maple syrup, and water. Bring to a boil and cook until the liquid has thickened, 30 to 60 seconds.

BUILD THE BOWLS

3 Spoon the warm grains into bowls. Top each with caramelized apples and sprinkle with granola. Serve with maple syrup and milk for drizzling.

1 batch cooked grains

Milk (unsweetened nut, coconut, soy, or regular milk), as needed

CARAMELIZED APPLES

2 tablespoons unsalted butter or virgin coconut oil, plus more for the grains

2 medium tart apples (such as Granny Smith), peeled, cored, and diced

Salt

½ teaspoon ground cinnamon

2 tablespoons maple syrup, plus more for serving

2 tablespoons water

TOPPING

Granola or coarsely chopped toasted walnuts, pecans, or almonds

MAKE-AHEAD OPTION

Refrigerate the apples for up to 5 days. Reheat before serving.

MILLET MUESLI

I'm a texture fanatic. Meaning, I like lots of it. That's why this bowl is one of my favorites: it's creamy, chewy, and crunchy, not to mention sweet, tart, and nutty (I'm also a flavor fanatic). While muesli is traditionally made with soaked oats, this version uses millet, one of my favorite breakfast grains — it's mild, with a subtle cornlike flavor and a couscouslike texture (with none of the gooeyness you sometimes get in oatmeal). Here it is simmered with cinnamon, shredded green apple, dried cherries, dates, and nuts for a breakfast that hits all the right notes.

SERVES 4 | PREP TIME: 5 minutes | COOKING TIME: 10–15 minutes

1 Shred half of the apple on the large holes of a box grater.

2 Place the millet in a medium pot with the shredded apple, cherries, dates, and cinnamon. Season with a pinch of salt. Add enough milk to loosen the mixture, and bring to a simmer. Cook until warmed through and fragrant, 10 to 15 minutes. Stir in a knob or two of butter, along with the nuts. Sweeten with maple syrup to taste.

3 Finely slice the remaining half of the apple.

4 Spoon the grains into bowls and top with the sliced apple and some more dried fruit. Serve with maple syrup and milk for drizzling.

1 green apple, halved and cored

1 batch cooked millet

⅓ cup dried cherries or cranberries, plus more for serving

⅓ cup chopped pitted dates, plus more for serving

½ teaspoon ground cinnamon

Salt

Milk (unsweetened nut, coconut, soy, or regular milk), as needed

Unsalted butter or virgin coconut oil, as needed

⅓ cup chopped toasted nuts (such as walnuts, almonds, cashews, and/or pecans)

Maple syrup, as needed

PEACHES & CREAM
+ CASHEW CREAM

CASHEW CREAM

1 cup raw cashews

1 or 2 pitted Medjool dates, coarsely chopped

⅛ teaspoon ground cardamom (optional)

1¼ cups water

Salt

BOWLS

1 batch cooked grains

2 ripe peaches, diced

Honey or maple syrup, for serving

Granola or coarsely chopped pecans, for serving

When I was a kid, my favorite way to eat fresh peaches was diced in a bowl with heavy cream splashed over the top. Today, I usually swap out the heavy cream for a lighter, dairy-free cashew cream, which is just as silky and rich but is surprisingly easy to make (just note that you need to soak the cashews for several hours or overnight). The touch of cardamom is optional, but if you haven't tried peaches with cardamom, it's a match made in heaven.

While the peaches and cashew cream are incredible on their own, you can turn them into a more substantial breakfast by serving them over warm grains with a speckling of granola or chopped nuts for texture. It almost tastes like a crisp, which just happens to be my second favorite way to eat peaches. The cashew cream is also delicious in smoothies and shakes.

SERVES 4 | PREP TIME: 10 minutes, plus 6–12 hours to soak the cashews

MAKE THE CASHEW CREAM

1 Place the cashews in a small bowl and cover with 1 to 2 inches of water. Let sit at room temperature for 6 to 12 hours.

2 Drain the cashews, and transfer them to a high-speed blender (such as a Vitamix). Add the dates (2 dates will give you a slightly sweeter cream), cardamom (if using), 1 cup of the water, and a pinch of salt. Blend on high speed until smooth. If needed, add some of the remaining ¼ cup water until the cashew cream has a rich, pourable consistency similar to heavy cream. Transfer to a bowl or jar.

BUILD THE BOWLS

3 If needed, reheat the grains in the microwave or on the stovetop (if using the stovetop, add a tablespoon or two of water). Spoon the warm grains into bowls and drizzle generously with the cashew cream. Top with the peaches and drizzle with honey. Garnish with a sprinkle of granola.

MAKE-AHEAD OPTION

Refrigerate the cashew cream for up to 5 days. It will thicken as it chills.

SUPERFOOD MORNING

I'm glad that wild blueberries are an antioxidant-rich superfood, because we go through several bags of them each week. We usually opt for frozen instead of fresh, as they're available year-round and are typically less expensive (although James and I still joke about our weekly "blueberry budget"). My kids eat the berries straight from the freezer by the bowlful, we blend them into smoothies, and we heat them up as a quick topping for pancakes, waffles, and breakfast bowls like this one.

These bowls are also topped with nutrient-rich chia seeds and goji berries, as well as coconut flakes and nuts for healthy fats. This is a vitamin- and mineral-packed way to super-start your day.

SERVES 4　|　PREP TIME: 5 minutes　|　COOKING TIME: 5 minutes

1 Place the grains in a medium pot and add the cinnamon and enough milk to loosen. Bring to a simmer. Stir in a spoonful or two of oil.

2 Spoon the warm grains into bowls and top with blueberries, goji berries, coconut flakes, chopped nuts, and a sprinkle of chia seeds. Serve with honey or maple syrup for drizzling.

1　batch cooked grains

½　teaspoon ground cinnamon

Milk (unsweetened nut, coconut, soy, or regular milk), as needed

Virgin coconut oil, as needed

1½　cups fresh or frozen wild blueberries (if using frozen, heat the berries in the microwave or on the stovetop until thawed)

TOPPINGS

Goji berries, for serving

Toasted unsweetened coconut flakes

Toasted chopped almonds, pecans, and/or cashews

Chia seeds, for serving

Honey or maple syrup, for serving

ROASTED RHUBARB & STRAWBERRIES
+ YOGURT & PISTACHIOS

ROASTED RHUBARB & STRAWBERRIES

- 3 tablespoons maple syrup
- 1 tablespoon packed light brown sugar
- 1 teaspoon vanilla extract
  Salt
- 2 cups diced rhubarb (3 or 4 stalks)
- 1 cup diced strawberries

BOWLS

- 1 batch cooked grains
  Plain yogurt (preferably whole-milk), for serving
  Chopped pistachios, for serving
  Honey or maple syrup, for serving

MAKE-AHEAD OPTION

The fruit can be refrigerated for up to 5 days. Reheat or serve cold.

Other Sauces to Try

- Strawberry-Chia Jam (page 42)

Strawberry-Chia Jam (page 42)

Have you ever tried roasting rhubarb? It's a total game-changer, resulting in a sweet, complex flavor without the need for tons of sugar. Here it is roasted with strawberries, maple syrup, a touch of brown sugar, and vanilla for a sauce that will take every ounce of your willpower not to devour with a spoon.

My daughter loves to swirl the roasted fruit into plain yogurt for a quick (and healthy, but *shh*) weeknight dessert. I follow her lead and serve the sauce with yogurt and a shower of pistachios over grains for breakfast. *Swoon!* You can roast the fruit up to five days in advance, and it is also fabulous on biscuits, pound cake, ice cream, pancakes, and waffles.

SERVES 4 | PREP TIME: 5 minutes | COOKING TIME: 40 minutes

MAKE THE ROASTED RHUBARB & STRAWBERRIES

1 Preheat the oven to 375°F (190°C). Line a rimmed baking sheet with parchment paper.

2 Combine the maple syrup, sugar, vanilla, and a pinch of salt in a small bowl. Stir until smooth.

3 Place the rhubarb and strawberries in a large bowl and pour the maple syrup mixture over them. Toss gently to coat. Scrape the fruit onto the prepared baking sheet and spread in a single layer. Roast for 30 to 35 minutes, stirring gently halfway through, until the rhubarb is very tender and the juices have reduced and look slightly syrupy (the edges will be a bit browned). Immediately transfer the fruit and juices to a bowl.

BUILD THE BOWLS

4 If needed, reheat the grains in the microwave or on the stovetop (if using the stovetop, add a tablespoon or two of water). Spoon the warm grains into bowls and top with a generous spoonful of the roasted rhubarb and strawberries (with their juices) as well as a large dollop of yogurt. Sprinkle each bowl with chopped pistachios. Serve with honey or maple syrup for drizzling.

PEANUT BUTTER & BERRY
+ STRAWBERRY-CHIA JAM

STRAWBERRY-CHIA JAM

- 2 cups coarsely chopped strawberries
- 2 tablespoons honey or agave nectar
- 1 teaspoon lemon juice
- 1½ tablespoons chia seeds

BOWLS

- 1 batch cooked grains

  Milk (unsweetened nut, coconut, soy, or regular milk), as needed

- 1–2 tablespoons honey or maple syrup, plus more for serving

  Nut butter, for serving

  Blueberries, for serving

  Coarsely chopped roasted salted peanuts, for serving

MAKE-AHEAD OPTION

Refrigerate the jam for up to 1 week.

Other Sauces to Try

- Roasted Rhubarb & Strawberries (page 40)

I love adding peanut butter to my favorite foods, from smoothies to sauces to brownies, and breakfast is no exception. These bowls are swirled with nut butter (use your favorite — see facing page for how to make your own) and then topped with a quick strawberry-chia jam.

If you've never made jam before, this is the recipe for you. It uses only four ingredients, and rather than adding pectin, you thicken the jam with chia seeds, which are packed with antioxidants, fiber, and omega-3 fatty acids. Talk about a win-win situation! I like to top the bowls with fresh blueberries and chopped peanuts for a pop of color and texture. Leftover jam is delicious on toast, in sandwiches, on yogurt, or over ice cream.

SERVES 4 | PREP TIME: 15 minutes | COOKING TIME: 20 minutes

MAKE THE JAM

1 Place the strawberries in a small pot. Cook over medium heat, stirring often with a rubber spatula, until the berries begin to break down and the mixture turns juicy and slightly foamy, 4 to 5 minutes. Using the spatula, gently smash some of the fruit.

2 Remove the pot from the heat and stir in the honey, lemon juice, and chia seeds. Put the pot back over medium heat and cook for 30 to 60 seconds.

3 Transfer the jam to a bowl or jar and let cool until completely thickened, about 10 minutes.

BUILD THE BOWLS

4 Place the grains in a medium pot and add enough milk to loosen. Bring to a simmer. Add the honey or maple syrup to taste.

5 Spoon the warm grains into bowls. Top each with a generous spoonful of nut butter, using a spoon to swirl it into the grains. Spoon some of the strawberry jam over each and top with a sprinkle of blueberries and peanuts. Serve with additional honey or maple syrup for drizzling.

PUMPKIN PIE RICE PUDDING

These bowls are like the love child of rice pudding and pumpkin pie, but they just happen to be naturally sweetened and nutritious. Best of all, with a batch of premade brown rice in the fridge, they come together in about 15 minutes. This is what you'll want to eat for breakfast the minute the trees start to change color (it's also one of my favorite afternoon snacks). You won't really taste the orange juice, but it brightens up and balances the flavors. And in case you were wondering, yes, pumpkins are technically a fruit!

SERVES 4 | PREP TIME: 5 minutes | COOKING TIME: 10 minutes

1 Pour the coconut milk into a medium pot and stir in the cinnamon, salt, ginger, cloves, nutmeg, pumpkin purée, banana purée, water, and vanilla. Bring the mixture to a boil over medium heat, stirring occasionally. Add the rice. Return the mixture to a simmer and let cook, stirring occasionally, until slightly thickened, 5 to 10 minutes. Mix in the maple syrup and orange juice.

2 Spoon the warm rice into bowls and drizzle with more maple syrup. Sprinkle with chopped pecans.

1 (14-ounce) can coconut milk

1 teaspoon ground cinnamon

½ teaspoon kosher salt

¼ teaspoon ground ginger

⅛ teaspoon ground cloves

⅛ teaspoon ground nutmeg

1 cup pumpkin purée (canned or homemade)

½ medium banana, mashed to a purée with a fork

¼ cup water

½ teaspoon vanilla extract

1 batch cooked brown rice

2 tablespoons maple syrup, plus more for serving

1 teaspoon orange juice

Chopped pecans, for serving

HOMEMADE PEANUT BUTTER

It's shockingly easy to make your own peanut butter, it's a *huge* cost saver and, best of all, you end up with the creamiest peanut butter ever, which doesn't separate in the fridge! You can make it in either a food processor or a high-speed blender like a Vitamix (a regular blender won't work).

Start with 2½ cups of roasted unsalted peanuts. If using a food processor, place the peanuts in the food processor and add ½ teaspoon kosher salt. Process until the peanuts turn smooth and glossy,

5 to 6 minutes (the nuts will clump up and form a ball before smoothing out).

If using a Vitamix, place the peanuts and ½ teaspoon kosher salt in the container, and secure the lid. Slide the tamper through the lid plug. Start the machine and slowly increase the speed to high, using the tamper to press the nuts into the blade. Keep working it until the peanut butter flows easily around the blade and turns glossy, 1 to 2 minutes.

SUNSHINE CITRUS
+ COCONUT CREAM

In the dead of winter, I crave breakfasts that are sunny and enlivening yet warm and comforting. This is just the meal for those chilly, dark mornings. Cooked grains are reheated with coconut milk, cinnamon, and cardamom, then topped with honey-scented citrus segments. A quick whipped coconut cream slowly melts into the bowls, providing velvety richness, while toasted almonds add texture. It's the ultimate dish to cheer up a dusky day.

SERVES 4 | **PREP TIME:** 10 minutes | **COOKING TIME:** 10–15 minutes

1 Open the can of coconut milk (don't shake it) and carefully spoon off ½ cup of the thick cream on the top. Put the cream in a medium bowl and place the bowl in the refrigerator.

2 Put the cooked grains in a medium saucepan and pour in the rest of the coconut milk and cream from the can. Stir in enough regular or nut milk so that the grains are loose but not watery. Add the cardamom pods, cinnamon stick, and a pinch of salt. Bring the mixture to a simmer and cook until the grains have just started to fall apart and the mixture is fragrant, 5 to 15 minutes.

3 In the meantime, using a sharp knife, cut off the top and bottom of the navel orange, just enough to expose the flesh. Place the orange, flat side up, on a cutting board and slice downward following the shape of the orange to remove the skin and pith. Cut in between the membranes to remove the orange segments. Transfer the segments to a bowl and repeat with the blood orange and grapefruit (transfer them to the same bowl). Fold in the honey.

4 Drizzle the vanilla over the cold coconut cream and whisk vigorously to combine (it's okay if the cream is still slightly lumpy, as it will melt into the bowls, but you can use handheld beaters for a smoother consistency).

5 Spoon the warm grains into bowls. Add a spoonful or two of the coconut cream and arrange the citrus segments over the top (also drizzle on any juices that have accumulated in the bowl). Sprinkle each bowl with toasted almonds. Serve with honey for drizzling.

1 (14-ounce) can full-fat coconut milk

1 batch cooked grains

Milk (unsweetened nut, coconut, soy, or regular milk), as needed

2 green cardamom pods, cracked with the side of a knife

1 cinnamon stick

Salt

1 medium navel orange

1 medium blood orange

1 large grapefruit

1 tablespoon honey, plus more for serving

1 teaspoon vanilla extract

¼ cup toasted sliced almonds

MAKE-AHEAD OPTION

You can segment the citrus 1 day ahead (don't add the honey). Store the segments in an airtight container in the refrigerator. Add the honey before proceeding.

TRIPLE-CHOCOLATE BUCKWHEAT

1¼ cups milk (unsweetened nut, coconut, soy, or regular milk), plus more as needed

2 tablespoons raw cacao powder or unsweetened cocoa powder

⅛ teaspoon ground cinnamon

Salt

3–4 tablespoons honey or agave nectar

½ teaspoon vanilla extract

1 batch cooked buckwheat

TOPPINGS

Berries of your choice

Sliced bananas

Coarsely chopped dark chocolate

Raw cacao nibs

Hemp seeds

These bowls are rich, chocolaty, *and* healthful. The nuttiness of buckwheat is the perfect match for chocolate, and this breakfast includes a triple dose: raw cacao powder, dark chocolate, and cacao nibs. The cacao powder, which is high in antioxidants, magnesium, and iron, lends a luxurious, hot-chocolate flavor (you could substitute regular unsweetened cocoa powder), while chopped dark chocolate and a sprinkle of cacao nibs provide a sweet-bitter punch.

The bowls are naturally sweetened with honey and are topped with berries and bananas. It's an antioxidant-rich way to kick off the day, plus chocolate! *For breakfast!*

SERVES 4 | PREP TIME: 5 minutes | COOKING TIME: 5–10 minutes

1 Pour the milk into a medium pot and whisk in the cacao powder, cinnamon, a pinch of salt, 3 tablespoons of the honey, and the vanilla. Place the pan over medium heat and bring the mixture to a simmer, whisking to dissolve the cacao powder and honey.

2 Add the buckwheat (if it's cold, break up the grains with a fork) and stir to combine. Bring to a simmer. Cook until warmed through, stirring occasionally. If it seems too thick, stir in another ¼ cup milk (alternatively, if it's too thin, let it simmer until slightly thickened). Give it a taste; add another tablespoon of honey if you prefer it sweeter.

3 Spoon the buckwheat into bowls. Top with berries and sliced bananas. Sprinkle with chopped dark chocolate, cacao nibs, and hemp seeds, if you'd like.

LOX & EGGS + CHIVE CRÈME FRAÎCHE, PAGE 58

④
EGGS

One of my earliest taste memories is my mom's fried egg sandwiches. She'd layer a runny egg between two pieces of Wonder bread (this was back in the 1980s) with American cheese, ketchup, and, on my request, grape jelly (don't ask). Regardless of my tastes (or lack thereof), what I really fell in love with was that golden, molten yolk. I still think that an egg makes nearly any dish better, and we go through a carton or more every week. They're an easy and fast source of healthy proteins and fats that my kids will reliably eat.

In these bowls, the egg in its many forms plays a starring role, from runny fried and poached eggs to creamy soft-boiled eggs to make-ahead hard-boiled eggs. You'll find a modern take on huevos rancheros, a classic interpretation of lox and eggs, spring pea bowls with soft-boiled eggs, and much more. These are meals that can be served for breakfast, lunch, or dinner, and while they're more sophisticated and nutritious than those bygone sandwiches, they're just as satisfying.

If possible, buy local pastured eggs, which will be fresher and more flavorful than supermarket brands. Oh, and if you don't eat eggs, there are several egg-free variations!

SOFT BOILED, HARD BOILED, POACHED & FRIED

SOFT-BOILED EGGS

Soft-boiled eggs have fully set whites and thick, jammy yolks. The longer the eggs sit in the water, the firmer the yolks will become, so choose the time according to your preference.

- 4–8 eggs

Arrange the eggs in a single layer in the bottom of a pot and cover with cold water by 1 inch. Bring the water to a boil. Once the water comes to a rolling boil, immediately remove the pot from the heat and cover. Let sit for 4 to 6 minutes.

Transfer the eggs to a bowl of ice water and chill just until the eggs are barely warm, about 2 minutes. Drain and peel.

HARD-BOILED EGGS

Forget that ugly gray ring around the yolk — these perfectly cooked hard-boiled eggs have a bright yellow yolk that's still slightly tender. A 12-minute egg will have a slightly firmer yolk than an 11-minute egg.

- 4–8 eggs

Arrange the eggs in a single layer in the bottom of a pot and cover with cold water by 1 inch. Bring the water to a boil. Once the water comes to a rolling boil, immediately remove the pot from the heat and cover. Let sit for 11 to 12 minutes.

Transfer the eggs to a bowl of ice water to stop the cooking. Once cool, drain and peel.

MAKE-AHEAD OPTION

Peeled soft-boiled eggs can be refrigerated for up to 3 days. Reheat in a pot of barely simmering water until slightly warm, about 1 minute.

MAKE-AHEAD OPTION

Unpeeled hard-boiled eggs can be covered and refrigerated for up to 1 week.

POACHED EGGS

Don't let poaching intimidate you! With a few simple steps, it's really no harder than frying. Use the freshest eggs you can find, as they hold their shape better. If you're using older eggs, crack each egg into a fine-mesh strainer and let the excess watery white run out before transferring the egg to a small bowl or ramekin (this will give the poached egg a more compact shape).

I usually poach my eggs in just water, but you can also add 1 to 2 teaspoons of white vinegar, which will help the whites set faster.

- 4 eggs
- Salt and freshly ground black pepper

Crack the eggs into 4 small bowls or ramekins. Fill a large straight-sided skillet or a wide pot with 3 inches of water. Place the pan over medium heat and bring the water to a very gentle simmer — you should see small, scattered bubbles.

Carefully slide an egg into the water, keeping the rim of the bowl right near the surface of the water (this will help the egg keep its shape). If needed, use a spoon to swirl the white around the yolk. Repeat with the other eggs, spacing them at least 1 to 2 inches apart.

Let the eggs cook at a gentle simmer, adjusting the heat as necessary, until the whites are set but the yolks are still jiggly, about 3 minutes. Using a slotted spoon, transfer the eggs to a plate or to your bowls, and season with salt and pepper to taste.

MAKE-AHEAD OPTION

The eggs can be poached 1 day ahead. As they come out of the water, transfer them to an ice bath. Cover the bowl and refrigerate the eggs (in the water). Before serving, transfer the eggs to a pot of barely simmering water until warmed through, about 1 minute.

FRIED EGGS

When it comes to fried eggs, there are two kinds of people — those who like crispy edges, and those who prefer silky whites. I'm fully nonpartisan and have therefore included recipes for both methods here. These are both sunny-side up, but if you prefer your eggs over-easy, use the "tender" method and give them a flip once the whites are set.

- Olive oil or unsalted butter, as needed
- 4 eggs
- Salt and freshly ground black pepper

FOR CRISPY WHITES: Heat a good amount of oil in a nonstick skillet (enough to fully coat) over medium-high heat. Once the oil is hot, crack in your eggs (cook only as many eggs as can fit in the pan without crowding). Cook, shaking the pan occasionally and using a rubber spatula to nudge the eggs apart, until the edges turn golden, about 2 minutes.

Tilt the pan and let the oil pool at the bottom. Using a spoon, baste the egg whites (not the yolks) with the hot oil until they are set but the yolks are still runny, about 1 minute longer. Season with salt and pepper to taste before serving.

FOR TENDER WHITES: Heat oil and/or butter in a nonstick skillet (just enough to lightly coat) over medium heat. Swirl to coat the pan. Crack in your eggs (it's okay if they touch).

Once the whites start to turn opaque, cover the pan and decrease the heat to low. Cook until the whites are set but the yolks are still runny, 3 to 4 minutes. Season with salt and pepper to taste before serving.

ASPARAGUS & EGGS
+ MISO BUTTER

MISO BUTTER

- 2 tablespoons unsalted butter, softened
- 2 tablespoons white miso
- ½ teaspoon grated fresh gingerroot

BOWLS

- 1 pound asparagus, tough ends trimmed

  Salt

- 2 cups cooked sorghum, brown rice, wheat berries, spelt berries, Khorasan wheat (Kamut), farro, or einkorn

- 2 scallions, thinly sliced

  Freshly ground black pepper

- 4 eggs

  Gochugaru or red pepper flakes, for serving (optional)

  Lemon wedges, for serving

GOCHU-WHAT?

Gochugaru is a blend of red chile pepper flakes used in Korean cooking. It's more complex than regular red pepper flakes, with a sweeter, fruitier, and slightly smokier flavor. Find it at specialty grocers or online.

I almost included double the quantity of the miso butter in this recipe, just so you would have extra in your fridge. It's salty in that indescribable umami kind of way, with a touch of sweetness and a hint of ginger. It immediately elevates nearly anything it touches. Try it on grains and noodles, steamed or roasted vegetables, corn on the cob, or sliced cucumbers. (Learn more about miso on page 162.)

Here it takes a simple mix of hearty grains and blanched asparagus into a whole new dimension. The grains and asparagus make for a lovely side dish on their own, but when topped with a runny egg, they become a crave-worthy meal. The recipe makes two large servings or four smallish servings (James and I usually have no trouble polishing this off on our own!).

SERVES 2–4 | PREP TIME: 10 minutes | COOKING TIME: 10 minutes

MAKE THE MISO BUTTER

1 Combine the butter, miso, and gingerroot in a small bowl. Using a rubber spatula, stir and mash everything together until smooth. The miso butter can be refrigerated for up to 2 weeks.

BUILD THE BOWLS

2 Bring a medium pot of water to a boil. Fill a large bowl with ice water. Cut the asparagus into 1-inch pieces, reserving the tips. Once the water reaches a boil, season it with salt. Add the asparagus stalks (not the tips). Cook for 1 minute, then add the tips. Continue cooking until the asparagus is bright green and tender crisp, 1 to 2 minutes longer, depending on the width of the asparagus. Drain and transfer to the bowl of ice water (this will stop the cooking and preserve the color). Drain again and pat dry.

3 If the grains are cold, reheat them in the microwave or on the stovetop (if using the stovetop, add 1 to 2 tablespoons of water). Stir in the miso butter and toss until coated. Fold in the asparagus and scallions. Season with salt and pepper.

4 Fry or poach the eggs. (See page 51.)

5 Divide the grains and asparagus into bowls. Top each with an egg and sprinkle with gochugaru, if using. Serve with lemon wedges.

HEARTY GREENS & GRAINS SALAD
WITH PANCETTA & POACHED EGGS

This is the kind of meal you will crave even if salad isn't usually your thing. A warm sherry vinegar and pancetta dressing and a runny poached egg soften the tough-guy persona of the sturdy greens, while grains, sweet peas, currants, toasted nuts, and shaved Parmesan provide a riot of texture and flavor.

For the greens, you'll want something robust, such as escarole or mature spinach (opt for the larger leaves in bunches as opposed to the baby greens, which are too tender). Depending on what I have on hand, I'll often swap out the pancetta for bacon, and/or sub in roasted butternut squash for the peas.

SERVES 4 | PREP TIME: 15 minutes | COOKING TIME: 25 minutes

MAKE THE DRESSING

1 Cook the pancetta in a medium skillet over medium-low heat, stirring occasionally, until browned and crisp. Using a slotted spoon, transfer it to paper towels to drain. Discard all but 1 tablespoon of fat from the skillet.

2 Pour in the oil and add the shallot. Cook over medium heat, stirring, until softened but not browned, about 2 minutes. Add the vinegar and stir, scraping up the browned bits on the bottom of the pan. Remove the pan from the heat and whisk in the mustard and maple syrup. Season with salt and pepper, and set the dressing aside.

BUILD THE BOWLS

3 Bring a small pot of water to a boil. Season it with salt and add the peas. Cook until the peas are bright green and tender, 2 to 4 minutes. Drain and rinse under cold water to stop the cooking.

4 Put the grains and escarole in a large bowl, along with the peas, currants, nuts, and cooked pancetta. Using a vegetable peeler, shave a good amount of Parmesan cheese over the top. Season with salt and pepper.

5 Start the water to poach the eggs (see page 51). Reheat the dressing and toss with the salad (toss well, so that everything is evenly coated). Mound the salad into bowls.

6 Poach the eggs. (See page 51). Place a poached egg onto each salad and season the eggs with a bit of salt and pepper before serving.

DRESSING

- 4 ounces pancetta or bacon, diced
- 3 tablespoons extra-virgin olive oil
- 1 small shallot, minced (about 3 tablespoons)
- 2 tablespoons sherry vinegar
- 2 teaspoons Dijon mustard
- 1 teaspoon maple syrup
- Salt and freshly ground black pepper

BOWLS

- Salt
- 1 cup fresh or frozen peas
- 2 cups cooked and cooled sorghum, wheat berries, spelt berries, Khorasan wheat (Kamut), farro, einkorn, or barley
- 5–6 cups torn escarole or mature spinach (not baby spinach)
- ¼ cup dried currants
- ½ cup coarsely chopped toasted hazelnuts or pecans
- Chunk of Parmesan cheese, for shaving
- Freshly ground black pepper
- 4 eggs

HUEVOS RANCHEROS
+ FRESH TOMATO SALSA

We rarely go out for brunch (why combine breakfast and lunch when you can have both?) but when we do, I prefer Mexican all the way. Huevos rancheros is my go-to dish, and this version is just as satisfying as the restaurant version, but lighter and brighter (plus, you can eat it in your pj's!).

You should definitely try millet here; its cornlike flavor mimics fresh tortillas. The grains are topped with melty cheddar cheese, flavor-packed black beans (the secret is to simmer the beans with aromatics in some of the liquid), a fried egg, and fresh tomato salsa. It's a meal that's just as delicious for breakfast as it is for dinner. Or, if you must, brunch.

For a vegan variation, use a nondairy cheese and omit the egg.

SERVES 4 | PREP TIME: 30 minutes | COOKING TIME: 10 minutes

MAKE THE SALSA

1 Place the tomatoes in a colander and toss them with the salt. Let sit for 10 to 15 minutes to drain. Meanwhile, rinse the diced onion in cold water (this helps to take away the oniony bite) and drain well.

2 Combine the drained tomatoes, onion, jalapeño, cilantro, oil, and lime juice in a medium bowl. Season with salt and pepper to taste.

SALSA

- 1 pound ripe tomatoes, cored, seeded, and finely diced
- ¼ teaspoon kosher salt, plus more as needed
- ¼ medium onion, finely diced
- ½ jalapeño, seeded and finely diced
- 2 tablespoons chopped fresh cilantro
- 1 teaspoon extra-virgin olive oil

  Juice of ½ lime

  Freshly ground black pepper

RECIPE CONTINUES

BEANS

1 (15-ounce) can black beans

2 tablespoons extra-virgin olive oil

¼ medium onion, finely diced

Salt and freshly ground black pepper

1 large garlic clove, minced

½ jalapeño, seeded and finely diced

½ teaspoon ground cumin

¼ teaspoon dried oregano

1 fresh cilantro sprig plus 2 tablespoons chopped

Juice from ½ lime

BOWLS

1 batch cooked millet

1 tablespoon unsalted butter (optional)

1 cup shredded sharp cheddar cheese

4 eggs

1 avocado, pitted, peeled, and diced

Hot sauce, for serving

Toasted pepitas, for serving

MAKE THE BEANS

3 Drain the black beans, reserving ¼ cup of the liquid from the can.

4 Heat the oil in a small pot over medium heat. Add the onion and season with salt and pepper. Cook, stirring occasionally, until golden, about 2 minutes. Add the garlic and jalapeño and cook, stirring, until softened and fragrant, about 30 seconds. Stir in the cumin and oregano. Add the black beans along with the reserved liquid from the can. Add the cilantro sprig. Reduce the heat to low and cook, stirring occasionally, for 5 minutes. Add the lime juice and season with salt and pepper to taste.

BUILD THE BOWLS

5 Reheat the millet in the microwave or on the stovetop (if using the stovetop, add 1 to 2 tablespoons of water). For a bit more flavor, stir in the butter.

6 Spoon the warm grains into bowls (you might not need the entire batch — save leftovers for breakfast bowls or lunches), and sprinkle each evenly with about ¼ cup of cheese. Divide the beans over the top.

7 Fry 4 eggs. (See page 51.) Slide an egg onto each bowl. Arrange the salsa and avocado over the top, and garnish with plenty of hot sauce, chopped cilantro, and toasted pepitas.

LENTILS, MUSHROOMS & ARUGULA
WITH EGGS & TRUFFLE OIL

Memorize this equation: mushrooms + lentils + runny egg yolk + truffle oil = *heaven*. It will get you through life's stressful moments and will save you when you think there's nothing to cook for dinner. I love lentils because they're delicious, cheap, nutritious, quick-cooking, and filling. You can make them in advance and even freeze them for down the line.

Any brown or green lentils will work here, but I especially love the small green Le Puy lentils from France, which are a bit less earthy than brown lentils and have a firmer texture. Seasoning the lentils while they're still warm helps them to absorb loads of flavor. Don't skimp on the salt and pepper.

For a vegan variation, swap out the egg for sliced avocado.

SERVES 4 | PREP TIME: 10 minutes | COOKING TIME: 25 minutes

1 Place the lentils in a medium pot with the water, smashed garlic clove, parsley sprig, and bay leaf. Bring to a boil, then reduce the heat to a simmer and cook until tender but not mushy (they should still have a slight bite), 15 to 20 minutes. Drain and transfer to a bowl. Toss with 1 tablespoon of the vinegar and 1 tablespoon of the olive oil, and season with salt and pepper to taste.

2 In the meantime, heat the remaining 2 tablespoons olive oil in a large skillet over medium-high heat. Add the mushrooms and toss to coat. Let cook, stirring occasionally, until tender and lightly browned, about 5 minutes. Add the shallot and minced garlic, and season with salt and pepper to taste. Cook, stirring, until fragrant and tender, about 1 minute. Drizzle in the remaining 1 tablespoon vinegar and toss to coat. Remove the pan from the heat and stir in the chopped parsley.

3 Spoon the grains into bowls. Arrange the mushrooms, lentils, and a mound of arugula over the grains. Drizzle with truffle oil and a touch more vinegar.

4 Fry or poach 4 eggs. (See page 51.) Slide an egg on top of each bowl. Season with salt and pepper to taste, and sprinkle with walnuts.

½ cup brown or green lentils (preferably Le Puy), rinsed and drained

2 cups water

3 garlic cloves, 1 smashed, 2 minced

1 fresh flat-leaf parsley sprig plus 1 tablespoon chopped

1 bay leaf

2 tablespoons sherry vinegar, plus more for serving

3 tablespoons extra-virgin olive oil

Salt and freshly ground black pepper

7–8 ounces shiitake mushrooms, stems discarded, caps sliced ¼ inch thick

½ medium shallot, minced

1 batch cooked grains

2 cups baby arugula

Truffle oil, for serving

4 eggs

Toasted chopped walnuts, for serving

MAKE-AHEAD OPTION

The dressed lentils can be refrigerated in an airtight container for up to 5 days.

LOX & EGGS
+ CHIVE CRÈME FRAÎCHE

CHIVE CRÈME FRAÎCHE

- ½ cup crème fraîche
- 1 tablespoon minced fresh chives
- ½ teaspoon lemon zest
- 1 teaspoon lemon juice
- Salt and freshly ground black pepper

BOWLS

- ½ small red onion, very thinly sliced
- 4 eggs
- 1 batch cooked grains
- 6–8 ounces lox or smoked salmon, thinly sliced
- 1 small avocado, pitted, peeled, and thinly sliced
- ½ small English cucumber, thinly sliced
- Capers, rinsed and drained, for serving

Other Sauces to Try
- Herbed Yogurt Sauce (page 157)

This is Sunday morning at its best, especially when enjoyed with a sprawled-out newspaper, a piping-hot pot of tea, and Miles Davis trumpeting in the background. Ahh. . . . Truthfully, that doesn't happen as often as I'd like (hello, kids), but this quick and easy meal still transports me to that special place, even if eaten at seven p.m.

I love lox and smoked salmon with cream cheese, but I *adore* them with this quick chive crème fraîche sauce, which is spiked with a hint of lemon zest. Cucumber and avocado balance out the salty salmon, and a fried egg takes things over the top. Pull on your robe, pour a cup of coffee — or better yet, a mimosa — and welcome in the weekend. Even if it's a Wednesday night.

SERVES 4 | PREP TIME: 15 minutes | COOKING TIME: 5 minutes

MAKE THE CHIVE CRÈME FRAÎCHE

1 Combine the crème fraîche, chives, lemon zest, and lemon juice in a bowl. Season with salt and pepper to taste.

BUILD THE BOWLS

2 Put the onion in a bowl of ice water and let soak for 10 minutes or so (this will reduce the onion's pungent bite). Drain. While the onion soaks, fry the eggs. (See page 51.)

3 Spoon the grains into bowls. Arrange the lox, avocado, and cucumber in each bowl. Spoon a dollop of the crème fraîche sauce over the lox. Slide an egg into each bowl. Top the bowls with the onion and capers.

GIVE YOUR ONIONS A BATH

You know how sometimes when you eat raw onion it sticks around all day like an unwelcome guest? Soaking onions in cold water after you cut them helps to remove the sulfurous compounds that give onions their funk, leaving them mellow, crunchy, and much friendlier.

ROASTED FENNEL & ASPARAGUS
WITH CRISPY CHICKPEAS & FRIED EGGS
+ SMOKY RED PEPPER SAUCE

This recipe came about accidentally one night as a throw-together supper and has since become a staple. I love roasting fennel and asparagus, not only because it's probably the easiest way to cook them but also because it turns the vegetables sweet and nutty. The sauce is like a sexy red dress, transforming the veggies from everyday standards to center-stage stunners (it's also great over chicken or fish, as well as slathered on burgers and sandwiches).

The bowls are topped with crispy chickpeas, which you'll have a hard time not devouring straight from the pan. I'm partial to quinoa for these bowls, but any grain will work.

For a vegan variation, swap out the egg for sliced avocado.

SERVES 4 | PREP TIME: 15 minutes | COOKING TIME: 20 minutes

MAKE THE SAUCE

1 Place the garlic in a mini food processor or high-speed blender and process until chopped. Add the roasted red peppers, pine nuts, paprika, and sugar. Season with salt and pepper to taste. Process until smooth, scraping down the sides as needed. Add the oil and process until combined. Taste and add additional salt, pepper, and/or sugar, if needed.

BUILD THE BOWLS

2 Preheat the oven to 425°F (220°C) with racks in the lower third and upper third of the oven. Line three baking sheets with aluminum foil.

3 Spread the chickpeas out on paper towels and pat dry. Transfer the chickpeas to a large bowl and add the paprika, granulated garlic, and sugar. Season with salt and pepper to taste, and toss with 1 tablespoon of the oil. Scrape the chickpeas onto one of the foil-lined baking sheets, spreading them in a single layer.

4 In the same bowl (no need to wash), toss the fennel with 1 tablespoon of the oil. Season with salt and pepper. Arrange the fennel on the second foil-lined baking sheet in a single layer.

SAUCE

- 1 garlic clove
- 1 cup coarsely chopped jarred roasted red peppers
- 3 tablespoons toasted pine nuts
- 1/8 teaspoon smoked paprika
- Pinch of sugar
- Salt and freshly ground black pepper
- 2 tablespoons extra-virgin olive oil

BOWLS

- 1 (15-ounce) can chickpeas, rinsed and drained
- 1/2 teaspoon smoked paprika
- 1/2 teaspoon granulated garlic
- 1/4 teaspoon sugar
- Salt and freshly ground black pepper
- 3 tablespoons extra-virgin olive oil
- 1 large fennel bulb, trimmed and cut into 1/2-inch wedges
- 1 bunch asparagus, tough ends trimmed
- 1 batch cooked grains
- 4 eggs

RECIPE CONTINUES

MAKE-AHEAD OPTION

Refrigerate the sauce for up to 5 days.

Other Sauces to Try

- Roasted Red Pepper & Cashew Sauce (page 108)
- Salsa Verde (page 150)
- Classic Pesto (page 79)
- Mint Pesto (page 65)
- Herbed Yogurt Sauce (page 157)

5 In the same bowl, toss the asparagus with the remaining 1 tablespoon oil. Season with salt and pepper. Spread the asparagus on the third foil-lined baking sheet in a single layer (if you don't have enough baking sheets, you can put the chickpeas and asparagus on the same sheet — you might just need to pull off the asparagus first).

6 Pop the fennel in the oven on the upper rack and roast for 5 minutes to get a jump-start. After 5 minutes, slide the asparagus and chickpeas onto the lower rack. Set a timer for 10 minutes. Once the timer goes off, pull out the asparagus (it should be browned in spots and tender — if not, let it cook for another few minutes).

Give the chickpeas a shake and flip over the fennel wedges. Roast the chickpeas and fennel for 5 to 10 minutes longer, until the chickpeas are starting to split and the fennel is lightly browned and tender (feel free to pull the chickpeas out earlier, if needed). Season the chickpeas with more salt once they come out of the oven.

7 Fry the eggs. (See page 51.)

8 Spoon the grains into bowls. Top with the roasted fennel and asparagus. Slide a fried egg on top and drizzle with the smoky red pepper sauce. Sprinkle each bowl with crispy chickpeas.

PREPPING FENNEL

To trim a whole fennel bulb, first cut off the stems and fronds (the feathery fronds are edible and can be used as you would any tender herb, or for garnish). Cut the bulb in half lengthwise. I usually peel off and discard the outermost layer of the fennel, which tends to be tough. You can either slice the fennel crosswise or cut it vertically into wedges, keeping some of the core intact so that it holds all of the layers together.

SWEET PEA DUO WITH SOFT-BOILED EGGS + PEA PESTO

This is one of my favorite meals ever, but especially in March, when warm weather still feels a mile away but I'm dying for something sunny and green. This quick pea pesto (which can be made with frozen peas, meaning you can whip it up year-round) gives fresh life to grains, especially when topped with more juicy peas and sugar snaps. Soft-boiled eggs lend just the right amount of comfort, while shaved Pecorino Romano provides a salty bite.

If you're using frozen peas, you can actually skip the blanching step and simply defrost the peas overnight in the refrigerator or at room temperature for a couple of hours (score!). I prefer these bowls with brown rice, but any hearty grain will do.

For a vegan variation, swap out the eggs and cheese for white beans and sliced avocado.

SERVES 4 | PREP TIME: 20 minutes | COOKING TIME: 5 minutes

MAKE THE PESTO

1 Bring a small pot of water to a boil, and season it with salt. Fill a bowl with ice water. Cook the peas in the boiling water until bright green and tender, 2 to 4 minutes. Drain and transfer to the ice water to stop the cooking. Drain again. Set aside 1½ cups of the peas to sprinkle over the bowls later.

2 Drop the garlic clove into a food processor with the blade running. Add the mint, pine nuts, and lemon juice. Process to a coarse paste. Add the peas (not the ones you set aside) and season with salt and pepper to taste. Process to a coarse paste, scraping down the sides as needed. With the blade running, drizzle in the oil until incorporated. Taste and season with additional salt and pepper, if needed.

BUILD THE BOWLS

3 Soft boil the eggs. (See page 50.) Cool and peel.

4 Spoon the grains into bowls. Add 1 to 2 spoonfuls of the pea pesto to each bowl and toss to coat the grains. Arrange the reserved peas, sugar snap peas, and soft-boiled eggs over the top. Season with salt and pepper to taste and drizzle with oil. Dollop with a bit more of the pea pesto. Shave some Pecorino Romano over each bowl and serve with lemon wedges.

PESTO

Salt

1 pound (3–3½ cups) fresh or frozen sweet peas

1 large garlic clove, peeled

1 cup lightly packed fresh mint leaves

¼ cup toasted pine nuts

2 tablespoons lemon juice

Freshly ground black pepper

2 tablespoons extra-virgin olive oil

BOWLS

4 eggs

1 batch cooked grains

2 cups (6 ounces) sugar snap peas, thinly sliced on the diagonal

Salt and freshly ground black pepper

Extra-virgin olive oil, for serving

Pecorino Romano cheese, for serving

Lemon wedges, for serving

MAKE-AHEAD OPTION

Refrigerate the pesto for up to 3 days.

Other Sauces to Try
- Mint Pesto (page 65)
- Classic Pesto (page 79)

ROASTED MUSHROOMS & SPRING PEAS
WITH EGGS & GOAT CHEESE + MINT PESTO

While I love all seasons, spring just might be my favorite, especially when fresh herbs appear in our garden. We have a big planter filled with mint, and we use the leaves throughout the warm months, to sprinkle over pastas and stir-fries, to eat out of hand, or to blend into sauces and marinades.

Here a quick mint pesto brightens up balsamic-roasted mushrooms and sweet green peas. The bowls are topped with an egg (cooked any way you prefer), crumbled goat cheese, and chopped pistachios. Oh, *yes*. (Did I mention that I love spring?)

For a vegan variation, swap out the fried eggs for cannellini beans and the goat cheese for diced avocado.

SERVES 4 | PREP TIME: 20 minutes | COOKING TIME: 25 minutes

MAKE THE PESTO

1 Drop the garlic clove into a food processor with the blade running. Add the mint, parsley, pine nuts, pepper flakes, lemon juice, and salt and black pepper to taste. Process to a coarse purée, stopping to scrape down the sides as needed. With the blade running, drizzle the water and then the oil through the feed tube to incorporate. Taste and season with additional salt and black pepper as needed.

BUILD THE BOWLS

2 Preheat the oven to 400°F (200°C). Line a baking sheet with aluminum foil.

3 Toss the mushrooms on the baking sheet with the shallot, garlic, oil, and vinegar. Season with salt and black pepper to taste. Spread in a single layer. Roast, stirring once or twice, for about 20 minutes, or until the mushrooms are tender and caramelized, and any liquid that has released has evaporated.

4 Bring a small pot of water to a boil and season with salt. Fill a bowl with ice water. Cook the peas in the boiling water until bright green and tender, 2 to 4 minutes. Drain and transfer to the ice water to stop the cooking. Drain again.

5 Fry, poach, or soft boil the eggs. (See pages 50–51.)

6 Spoon the grains into bowls. Arrange the mushrooms and peas over each bowl. Slide an egg onto each bowl. Drizzle with the mint pesto and top with the goat cheese and chopped pistachios.

PESTO

- 1 garlic clove, peeled
- 1½ cups lightly packed fresh mint leaves
- 1 cup lightly packed fresh flat-leaf parsley
- ¼ cup toasted pine nuts
- ⅛ teaspoon red pepper flakes
- 1 tablespoon lemon juice

  Salt and freshly ground black pepper
- 2 tablespoons water
- 6 tablespoons extra-virgin olive oil

BOWLS

- 1 pound cremini or assorted wild mushrooms, sliced ¼ inch thick
- 1 medium shallot, finely diced
- 2 garlic cloves, minced
- 2 tablespoons extra-virgin olive oil
- 1 tablespoon balsamic vinegar

  Salt and freshly ground black pepper
- 1½ cups fresh or frozen peas
- 1 batch cooked grains
- 4 eggs
- 4 ounces goat cheese, crumbled
- ¼ cup toasted pistachios

ROASTED SWEET POTATOES & BRUSSELS SPROUTS
WITH EGGS & MAPLE PECANS + MAPLE-SRIRACHA YOGURT

When I originally wrote this recipe, I planned on cooking everything on the stovetop, but then I went to test it after a particularly crazy day and didn't have the energy to tend to a bunch of skillets. Instead, I threw everything in the oven, and the result was way tastier, easier, and less messy than the original plan (no grease-splattered stove!).

Roasted sweet potatoes and Brussels sprouts are piled over grains and topped with runny eggs and a one-minute maple-sriracha yogurt sauce, which you're going to want to slather over everything (including the Deconstructed (and Lightened-Up) Pork Tenderloin Banh Mi Bowls on page 126). Crispy maple pecans take these bowls over the top. So go ahead and pour yourself a glass of wine and unwind while the oven does its thing.

For a vegetarian variation, omit the bacon.

SERVES 4 | PREP TIME: 15 minutes | COOKING TIME: 45 minutes

MAKE THE MAPLE-SRIRACHA YOGURT

1 Mix together the yogurt, sriracha, and maple syrup to taste in a small bowl. Season with salt and pepper to taste.

BUILD THE BOWLS

2 Preheat the oven to 400°F (200°C). Line one baking sheet with parchment paper and two baking sheets with aluminum foil.

3 Pour the pecans onto the parchment-lined baking sheet and drizzle with 1 tablespoon of the maple syrup. Sprinkle with the cinnamon and season with salt to taste. Toss well to coat, then spread the nuts in a single layer. Bake for 5 to 7 minutes, until the nuts are a shade darker in color and aromatic. Sprinkle with a bit more salt and let cool (the nuts will harden as they cool).

4 In the meantime, combine the Brussels sprouts and sweet potato on a foil-lined baking sheet and drizzle with the oil and the remaining 2 teaspoons maple syrup. Season with salt and pepper to taste and toss to coat. Spread in a single layer. Roast, stirring once or twice, for 35 to 40 minutes, until caramelized and tender.

MAPLE-SRIRACHA YOGURT

- 1 cup plain yogurt (preferably whole-milk)
- 2–3 teaspoons sriracha
- 2–3 teaspoons maple syrup
- Salt and freshly ground black pepper

BOWLS

- 1 cup pecans
- 1 tablespoon plus 2 teaspoons maple syrup
- ⅛ teaspoon ground cinnamon
- Salt
- 1 pound Brussels sprouts, trimmed and halved (or quartered if large)
- 1 medium sweet potato (1 pound), cut into ½-inch dice
- 2 tablespoons extra-virgin olive oil
- Freshly ground black pepper
- 4–8 bacon strips (optional)
- 4 eggs
- 1 batch cooked grains

RECIPE CONTINUES

MAKE-AHEAD OPTIONS

Refrigerate the sauce for up to 5 days.

Other Sauces to Try
- Creamy Chipotle Sauce (page 106)

5 While the vegetables cook, arrange the bacon (if using) on the second foil-lined baking sheet in a single layer. Slide the bacon into the oven with the vegetables and let bake for 15 to 18 minutes, until crisp (thick-cut bacon will take a few minutes longer). Transfer the bacon to paper towels to drain.

6 Fry or poach the eggs. (See page 51.)

7 Spoon the grains into bowls. Arrange the roasted vegetables on top of the grains, and slide an egg over the top of each. Drizzle with the yogurt sauce. Top with a strip or two of bacon, if using, and crush some maple pecans over the top.

MAPLE PECANS

This recipe makes more maple pecans than you'll likely need (if you don't end up snacking on them, as I inevitably do). Use leftovers on salads, over ice cream, or in desserts. They also make for a tasty snack alongside cocktails! Store in the refrigerator for up to 1 week.

VEGETABLE & QUINOA FRY-UP WITH EGGS

2 tablespoons extra-virgin olive oil

2 large garlic cloves, thinly sliced

1 small shallot, halved and thinly sliced

2 medium carrots, thinly sliced on the diagonal

¼ teaspoon ground Aleppo pepper or pinch of red pepper flakes

Salt and freshly ground black pepper

1 bunch Swiss chard, thick bottom stems discarded, leaves and upper stems thinly sliced

1 batch cooked quinoa

Juice of 1 lime

4 eggs

1 avocado, pitted, peeled, and thinly sliced

Hot sauce, for serving

Toasted pepitas or sunflower seeds, for serving

Other Sauces to Try
- Smoky Red Pepper Sauce (page 61)
- Creamy Chipotle Sauce (page 106)
- Tahini Sauce (page 94)
- Roasted Red Pepper & Cashew Sauce (page 108)

I started making these quick quinoa fry-ups for myself on the weekends as a way to get rid of leftover odds and ends in the vegetable drawer. One day James stole a few bites of the vegetables from the pan when I wasn't looking. The next week he asked me to make extra to go with his egg sandwich. The following week he ditched the egg sandwich altogether and made a big batch of this for both of us, and I didn't have to lift a finger. Talk about a win!

This is one of our favorite clean-out-the-fridge meals, and I hope it will become one of yours as well. We usually use carrots and greens, because that's inevitably what we have, but you can get creative using whatever is in your crisper. And while I usually make this with quinoa, it's great with any grain. Top the bowls with toasted seeds and the sauce of your choice.

For a vegan variation, swap out the egg for hummus or beans.

SERVES 4 | PREP TIME: 10 minutes | COOKING TIME: 20 minutes

1 Heat the oil in a very large skillet over medium-high heat. Add the garlic and shallot and cook, stirring occasionally, until they start to soften and smell fragrant, 1 to 2 minutes. Add the carrots and Aleppo pepper, and season with salt and black pepper. Toss to coat. Cook, stirring occasionally, until the carrots are slightly softened, 2 to 3 minutes.

2 Pile in the Swiss chard and season with a touch more salt and black pepper. Cook, stirring occasionally, until the chard is wilted and tender, 2 to 3 minutes. Stir in the quinoa and cook, stirring, for 1 to 2 minutes. Remove the skillet from the heat and add the lime juice. Season with salt and black pepper to taste.

3 Fry or poach the eggs. (See page 51.)

4 Spoon the quinoa and vegetable mixture into bowls and top each with an egg and some avocado slices. Drizzle with hot sauce and sprinkle with pepitas.

SWISS CHARD

Unlike kale, the stems of Swiss chard are perfectly edible. I discard the thick bottom portions, which tend to be fibrous, but slice up the remaining stems right along with the leaves. They add a nice crunch.

ROASTED BEETS, CARROTS & CAULIFLOWER WITH SPINACH, PAGE 89

VEGETABLES

I have a confession to make: I stink at gardening. When we moved to the Hudson Valley years ago, I had romantic images of myself spending hours in the new garden beds we dug out of our steep hillside, but it turns out that I couldn't even keep the rosemary in my kitchen window alive. Thank goodness my husband has a green thumb. He took over the tending of the plants, and I harvest and cook the produce. It's a good system, especially as I get to focus on doing what I love best — cooking vegetables. There's something so satisfying about working with (and eating) a palette of bright colors and varying textures.

These recipes are some of my favorite things to make and eat, from hearty salads that will make you rethink the versatility of grains to a quick curry and fried rice to produce-packed bowls that even picky eaters will devour. Whether you whip them up for a gorgeous lunch or a healthy dinner, I hope you'll love them as much as I do.

BALSAMIC-ROASTED MUSHROOMS & BRUSSELS SPROUTS
WITH GOAT CHEESE + GREMOLATA

GREMOLATA

- ¼ cup toasted pine nuts
- ½ cup lightly packed fresh flat-leaf parsley leaves and tender stems
- Zest of 1 lemon
- 1 garlic clove, coarsely chopped
- Salt and freshly ground black pepper

BOWLS

- 1 pound Brussels sprouts, trimmed and halved (quartered if large)
- 2 tablespoons extra-virgin olive oil, plus more for drizzling
- Salt and freshly ground black pepper
- 8 ounces cremini mushrooms, trimmed and quartered
- 2 teaspoons balsamic vinegar, plus more for drizzling
- 2–3 cups baby arugula or microgreens
- 1 batch cooked grains
- Goat cheese, for serving

Other Sauces to Try
- Classic Pesto (page 79)
- Sun-Dried Tomato Pesto (page 102)

Gremolata is an Italian chopped herb condiment — usually made with parsley, lemon zest, and garlic — that's traditionally spooned over braised meats (think osso buco). It adds instant bling to any dish it encounters, from roasted chicken to grilled lamb to fish and vegetables. It's particularly delicious in these bowls of earthy, roasted balsamic mushrooms, caramelized Brussels sprouts, and creamy goat cheese.

You'll want to start the vegetables first, then make the gremolata while they roast. For a bit more substance, slide a poached or fried egg over the top.

For a vegan variation, omit the cheese.

SERVES 4 | PREP TIME: 10 minutes | COOKING TIME: 25 minutes

MAKE THE GREMOLATA

1. Pile the pine nuts, parsley, lemon zest, and garlic on a cutting board. Chop everything together until the parsley is finely chopped. Transfer to a bowl and season with salt and pepper to taste.

BUILD THE BOWLS

2. Preheat the oven to 425°F (220°C). Line two baking sheets with aluminum foil.

3. Place the Brussels sprouts on one of the baking sheets and drizzle with 1 tablespoon of the oil. Season with salt and pepper, and toss to coat. Spread in a single layer.

4. Place the mushrooms on the second baking sheet and drizzle with the vinegar and the remaining tablespoon oil. Season with salt and pepper, and toss to coat. Spread in a single layer.

5. Roast the vegetables, stirring once or twice, for 15 to 20 minutes for the mushrooms and 20 to 25 minutes for the Brussels sprouts, until browned and tender.

6. Drizzle the arugula with a bit of vinegar and oil, and season with salt and pepper to taste. Toss to coat.

7. Spoon the grains into bowls. Arrange the Brussels sprouts, mushrooms, and arugula over each bowl and sprinkle with the gremolata. Crumble some goat cheese over each bowl.

FRIED "RICE"
WITH BROCCOLI, BABY SPINACH, AVOCADO & CASHEWS

Fried rice was one of my favorite dishes as a kid, and this vegetable-loaded version tastes even better than the greasy takeout I remember. And you don't even need to use rice! It's just as good with millet, quinoa, or even farro. The grains are stir-fried with broccoli, red bell pepper, spinach, gingerroot, garlic, and scallions. The bowls are topped with avocado for creaminess, toasted cashews for crunch, and sriracha or gochujang sauce for heat. I also like to add a spoonful of kimchi.

You'll need a wok or a 12-inch skillet with a lid (or just cover the skillet with a baking sheet). Be sure to prep all of the ingredients before beginning, as the cooking process goes quickly.

For a vegan variation, swap out the eggs for chopped tofu.

SERVES 4 | **PREP TIME:** 20 minutes | **COOKING TIME:** 10 minutes

1 Heat 1 tablespoon of the vegetable oil in a large wok or 12-inch skillet over medium-high heat until shimmering. Swirl the oil to evenly coat the pan. Pour in the eggs and gently shake the pan to create a thin layer along the bottom. Season with salt and pepper. Cook until the eggs are set on the bottom, 30 to 60 seconds. Flip the omelet and cook until set on the other side (if it sticks or breaks, don't worry — it will get cut up anyway). Slide the omelet onto a cutting board. Let it cool slightly, then cut it into thin strips.

2 Wipe out the wok, then add another tablespoon of the vegetable oil. Place the pan over high heat. Once the oil is shimmering, add the broccoli and bell pepper. Season with salt and pepper, and toss to coat. Cover and cook, stirring occasionally, until the broccoli is lightly browned, 3 to 4 minutes. Add the spinach and cook, stirring, until mostly wilted.

3 Push the vegetables to one side of the wok and pour the toasted sesame oil into the other side. Add the garlic, scallions, and gingerroot to the side with the sesame oil. Cook, stirring, until fragrant, about 30 seconds. Stir everything together. Add the remaining 1 tablespoon vegetable oil and the cooked grains. Cook, stirring, until the grains are coated and warmed through. Stir in the tamari and fold in the sliced eggs. Season with salt and pepper to taste.

4 Divide the fried rice among bowls. Top each bowl with avocado slices, cashews, scallions, and kimchi, if using. Serve with sriracha for drizzling.

3 tablespoons neutral vegetable oil (such as grapeseed)

2 eggs, beaten

Salt and freshly ground black pepper

1 small bunch broccoli (1 pound), cut into small florets (about 3 cups chopped)

½ red bell pepper, diced

2 cups baby spinach

1 tablespoon toasted sesame oil

3 large garlic cloves, minced

2 scallions, thinly sliced, plus more for serving

1 tablespoon minced fresh gingerroot

1 batch cooked quinoa, rice, millet, or farro (cooled)

1 tablespoon low-sodium tamari or soy sauce

TOPPINGS

2 small avocados, pitted, peeled, and thinly sliced

½ cup coarsely chopped toasted cashews

Kimchi (optional)

Sriracha or Gochujang Sauce (page 137)

DOUBLE-BROCCOLI POWER BOWLS
WITH CHICKPEAS & FENNEL

1 large bunch broccoli, cut into small florets and stems (5–6 cups chopped)

1 large garlic clove, peeled

⅔ cup toasted almonds

½ cup grated Parmesan cheese, plus shaved Parmesan for serving

2 tablespoons lemon juice, plus more as needed

Pinch of ground Aleppo pepper or red pepper flakes

Salt and freshly ground black pepper

7 tablespoons extra-virgin olive oil

1 cup chickpeas (rinsed and drained)

1 medium fennel bulb, shaved or very thinly sliced

1 batch cooked grains

1 avocado, pitted, peeled, and thinly sliced

My love of broccoli came late in life. I tried to avoid it as a kid (unless it was served with Cheez Whiz — oh, to be a child of the '80s), and then, much like laundry, made the best of it as a young adult. But when I became pregnant with Juniper, I suddenly fell in love with broccoli, and the romance hasn't diminished. When Heidi Swanson posted a recipe for Double-Broccoli Quinoa on 101cookbooks.com, I was immediately intrigued. She used broccoli two ways: in a pesto and steamed, and then tossed both with quinoa. Brilliant!

I've adapted her technique, and this is now one of my favorite ways to get my fix. Even if you're not as broccoli obsessed, I think you're going to love the pesto, which is cheesy, nutty, mild, and heartily approved by my two little rug rats (it's also delicious with pasta).

SERVES 4 | PREP TIME: 15 minutes | COOKING TIME: 20 minutes

1 Add about 1 inch of water to a medium pot and insert a steamer basket. Bring the water to a simmer. Add the broccoli and cover. Cook until bright green and tender crisp, 3 to 5 minutes. Drain and then rinse under cold water to stop the cooking.

2 Drop the garlic clove into a food processor with the blade running. Add ⅓ cup of the almonds and process until coarsely chopped. Add 3 cups of the steamed broccoli, along with the grated Parmesan cheese, 1 tablespoon of the lemon juice, and pinch of Aleppo pepper. Season with salt and black pepper. Process to a paste, scraping the sides as needed.

3 With the machine running, slowly drizzle in 6 tablespoons of the oil and process until combined. Taste and season with additional salt, black pepper, or lemon juice, if needed.

4 Combine the chickpeas and fennel in a medium bowl and toss with the remaining 1 tablespoon lemon juice and 1 tablespoon oil. Season with salt and black pepper to taste.

5 Coarsely chop the remaining ⅓ cup almonds.

6 Spoon the grains into bowls. Add 1 or 2 spoonfuls of the broccoli pesto to each bowl and toss to lightly coat the grains. Arrange the remaining steamed broccoli and the chickpea and fennel salad over the top. Add another spoonful of pesto. Top with the sliced avocado, chopped almonds, and shaved Parmesan.

For a kid-friendly version, serve all the ingredients in separate piles with a little bowl of sauce for dipping.

GREEN BEANS & GRAINS
WITH PARMESAN-CRUSTED ZUCCHINI, ROASTED TOMATOES & MOZZARELLA + CLASSIC PESTO

I'm convinced that Ella was Italian in a past life, and these bowls are dedicated to her. Parmesan-crusted zucchini coins are served over grains with green beans and pesto (I often substitute pasta for the kids). Juicy roasted tomatoes offer a sweet-tart punch, and fresh mozzarella lends creaminess. For a faster version, use thawed frozen peas in place of the green beans.

SERVES 4 | **PREP TIME:** 30 minutes | **COOKING TIME:** 20 minutes

MAKE THE PESTO

1 Drop the garlic clove into a food processor with the blade running. Add the basil, pine nuts, Parmesan, and lemon juice, and season with salt and pepper. Process until finely chopped, scraping down the sides as needed. With the blade running, slowly pour the oil through the feed tube and process until incorporated. Taste and season with additional salt, pepper, or lemon juice, if needed.

BUILD THE BOWLS

2 Preheat the oven to 400°F (200°C). Line two baking sheets with aluminum foil.

3 Place the zucchini, garlic, and oregano in a large bowl and toss with 2 tablespoons of the oil. Season with salt and pepper. Arrange the zucchini in a single layer on one of the baking sheets. Divide the Parmesan evenly over each zucchini round.

4 Arrange the tomatoes on the second baking sheet and drizzle with the remaining 1 tablespoon oil. Season with salt and pepper, and toss to coat. Roast the vegetables, stirring the tomatoes once or twice, for 15 to 20 minutes, until the tomatoes are tender and start to pop open and the zucchini is lightly browned.

5 In the meantime, add about 1 inch of water to a medium pot and insert a steamer basket. Bring the water to a simmer. Add the green beans, cover, and cook until the beans are bright green and tender crisp, 4 to 6 minutes. Drain and rinse under cold water to stop the cooking. Pat dry.

6 Place the grains and green beans in a large bowl and add ⅓ to ½ cup of the pesto (enough to coat the grains). Season with salt and pepper to taste, and toss to coat. Spoon the grains and beans into bowls, and arrange the zucchini, tomatoes, and bocconcini over the top. Serve with the remaining pesto.

PESTO

- 1 large garlic clove, peeled
- 2 cups lightly packed fresh basil leaves
- ¼ cup toasted pine nuts
- ½ cup grated Parmesan or Pecorino Romano cheese, or a mix of both
- Juice of ½ lemon, plus more as needed
- Salt and freshly ground black pepper
- ½ cup extra-virgin olive oil

BOWLS

- 2 medium zucchini (about 12 ounces), trimmed and sliced into ¼-inch-thick rounds
- 1 garlic clove, minced
- ¼ teaspoon dried oregano
- 3 tablespoons extra-virgin olive oil
- Salt and freshly ground black pepper
- ¼ cup grated Parmesan cheese
- 1 pint grape tomatoes
- 8 ounces green beans, trimmed and cut on the diagonal into 1-inch pieces
- 1 batch cooked grains
- 1 cup bocconcini (mini mozzarella balls), halved

GRILLED EGGPLANT, FENNEL & ARUGULA SALAD WITH FETA & MINT

- 1 medium Italian eggplant (about 1 pound), cut crosswise into ½-inch-thick slices
- ¼ cup extra-virgin olive oil, plus more for brushing the eggplant
- 1 tablespoon balsamic vinegar

  Salt and freshly ground black pepper
- ¼ cup lemon juice
- 1 garlic clove, minced or grated on a Microplane
- 2 cups cooked grains (cooled)
- 1 medium fennel bulb (about 1 pound), trimmed and sliced very thin on a mandoline or using a sharp knife
- 2 cups baby arugula
- ⅓ cup coarsely chopped fresh mint
- ⅓ cup toasted pine nuts

  Shaved Pecorino Romano cheese or crumbled feta cheese, for serving

  Pomegranate seeds, for serving

My favorite way to cook eggplant is on the grill, where it develops a slightly smoky flavor and a silky texture (see grilling tips, opposite). While it's hard not to gobble up grilled eggplant slices on their own, they also make for a wonderful addition to pastas and salads. This version incorporates shaved fennel, arugula, grains, toasted pine nuts, and fresh mint, along with salty Pecorino Romano or feta cheese and sweet-tart pomegranate seeds. I call it my Ottolenghi salad, after food writer and restaurateur Yotam Ottolenghi, who taught me that eggplants + pomegranate seeds + mint = BFF.

When shopping for eggplants, choose ones that are firm and heavy for their size, with smooth, taut skin — avoid any that are soft or saggy, as they tend to be bitter.

For a vegan variation, omit the cheese.

SERVES 4 | PREP TIME: 30 minutes | COOKING TIME: 10 minutes

1 Preheat a grill or grill pan to medium-high heat.

2 Brush the eggplant slices on both sides with oil. Drizzle with the vinegar. Season the slices on both sides with salt and pepper.

3 Grill the eggplant slices until browned with grill marks on both sides, 3 to 4 minutes per side. Transfer the slices to a plate, stacking them on top of one another in little piles. Cover tightly with aluminum foil and let sit for 10 minutes (this will allow the eggplant to steam and finish cooking through).

4 Combine the lemon juice and garlic in a small bowl. Whisk in the remaining ¼ cup oil and season with salt and pepper to taste.

5 Coarsely chop the eggplant.

6 Combine the grains, chopped eggplant, fennel, arugula, mint, and pine nuts in a large bowl. Drizzle with the dressing (you might not need it all) and toss to coat. Season with salt and pepper to taste. Sprinkle the salad with cheese and pomegranate seeds.

MAKE-AHEAD OPTION

The dressing can be refrigerated for up to 1 week. Bring to room temperature before serving.

GRILLING EGGPLANT

Eggplant has a reputation for being a bit tricky (and sticky) on the grill, but with the right tips, it's a cinch. First, brush the slices evenly with oil on both sides so that all the surfaces are coated — the eggplant will soak up the oil, but that's okay. Second, make sure your grill is nice and hot. Third, clean your grates! If the grill is clean and properly seasoned, then you're good to go. If not, clean it as best as you can, and brush the grates lightly with oil.

Arrange the eggplant slices on the grill and let them cook (covered if using an outdoor grill) until they lift easily from the grates and have developed grill marks. Flip and do the same on the other side. Finally, once the slices come off the grill, stack them into little piles and cover them with aluminum foil. This will allow the eggplant to steam and cook all the way through, developing a consistent texture.

GRILLED PEPPER & SWEET CORN SALAD
+ CREAMY AVOCADO-LIME DRESSING

DRESSING

- 1 medium avocado, pitted and peeled
- 1 garlic clove, coarsely chopped
- 1 small scallion, thinly sliced
- ½ jalapeño, seeds and ribs discarded
- ¼ cup lightly packed fresh cilantro leaves
- ¼ cup water
- ¼ cup neutral vegetable oil (such as grapeseed)
- 2 tablespoons lime juice
- 2 tablespoons rice vinegar
- ½ teaspoon honey

  Salt and freshly ground black pepper

BOWLS

- 1 medium red bell pepper, quartered
- 1 medium yellow bell pepper, quartered
- 1 tablespoon extra-virgin olive oil

  Salt and freshly ground black pepper

- 2 ears corn
- 2 cups cooked grains (cooled)
- 1 romaine heart, coarsely chopped
- 2 scallions, thinly sliced

  Toasted pepitas, for serving

  Crumbled cotija or feta cheese, for serving

This is the salad of my dreams. Lightly charred sweet peppers and grilled corn are tossed with romaine lettuce, grains, toasted pepitas, crumbled cotija or feta cheese, and a creamy (but dairy-free) avocado-lime dressing. It's the kind of meal that begs to be eaten outdoors. We whip it up for weekend lunches in the summer, or serve it alongside barbecued chicken or fish for dinner.

You can even grill the vegetables, make the dressing, and cook the grains during the weekend, then throw the salad together in seconds later in the week. Your weekday self will thank you!

For a vegan variation, omit the cheese.

SERVES 4 | PREP TIME: 25 minutes | COOKING TIME: 15 minutes

MAKE THE DRESSING

1 Combine the avocado, garlic, scallion, jalapeño, cilantro, water, vegetable oil, lime juice, vinegar, and honey in a blender and season with salt and pepper. Blend on high speed until smooth (there might still be some small chunks, and that's okay). Taste and adjust the seasonings as needed.

BUILD THE BOWLS

2 Preheat a grill to medium-high.

3 Drizzle the red and yellow bell peppers with the olive oil, rubbing on all sides to coat the peppers. Season with salt and black pepper.

4 Discard the dark green outer husks of the corn, leaving the inner husks intact. Peel back the inner husks halfway and pull off the silk. Wrap the cobs back in their husks.

5 Arrange the bell peppers and corn on the grill. Cook, flipping the peppers and turning the corn occasionally, until the peppers are lightly charred on both sides and the corn kernels are bright yellow and lightly toasted, 8 to 10 minutes total. Transfer the vegetables to a cutting board. Coarsely chop the peppers and cut the corn kernels off the cobs. Let cool.

6 Place the vegetables in a large bowl, and add the grains, lettuce, and scallions. Toss with just enough dressing to coat (you won't need it all). Season with salt and black pepper to taste. Top with pepitas and cheese. Serve with the remaining dressing on the side.

Other Sauces to Try
- Cumin Vinaigrette (page 97)

GREEK GOODNESS SALAD

DRESSING

- ¼ cup red wine vinegar
- 1 large garlic clove, finely minced or grated
- ½ teaspoon dried oregano

  Sea salt and freshly ground black pepper
- ½ cup extra-virgin olive oil

BOWLS

- ¼ medium red onion, very thinly sliced
- 1 medium fennel bulb, stalks discarded, fronds reserved, bulbs shaved or very thinly sliced
- 1 pint cherry or grape tomatoes, quartered or halved
- 1 medium English cucumber, halved and very thinly sliced
- ½ cup pitted kalamata olives, halved
- 2 cups cooked and cooled grains
- ¼ cup finely chopped fresh parsley
- ¼ cup finely chopped fresh mint
- 4–6 ounces feta cheese, crumbled, plus more for serving

This hearty Greek salad swaps out lettuce for crunchy shaved fennel and is packed with cherry tomatoes, cucumbers, olives, feta, and fresh herbs. The addition of a hearty grain turns it into a full meal. It's one of my favorite lunches, and it also makes a lovely side dish to accompany simple grilled lamb chops, fish, or kabobs (chicken, lamb, or shrimp).

SERVES 6 | PREP TIME: 15 minutes

MAKE THE DRESSING

1 Combine the vinegar, garlic, oregano, and a pinch of salt and pepper in a small bowl or jar. Let sit for 5 to 10 minutes to allow the flavors to meld. Add the oil and whisk or shake to combine.

BUILD THE BOWLS

2 Put the sliced onion in a small bowl and cover with hot water. Let sit while assembling the rest of the ingredients (this step isn't necessary, but it will take the "bite" out of the onion).

3 Combine the fennel, tomatoes, cucumber, olives, grains, parsley, mint, and feta (to taste) in a large bowl. Drain and rinse the onion in cold water, and add it to the bowl.

4 Season the salad with salt and pepper. Whisk or shake the dressing to combine. Drizzle about three-quarters of the dressing over the salad. Toss to coat. Taste and add more dressing if needed.

5 Spoon the salad into bowls and garnish with more feta and the reserved fennel fronds.

MAKE-AHEAD OPTION

The dressing can be made up to 2 days in advance. Bring to room temperature before using.

KALE CLEANSE SALAD
WITH COCONUT, GREEN APPLE & AVOCADO + LIME VINAIGRETTE

A couple of times a year, I need a reboot. Usually this happens in the fall and spring, when the shifting weather brings its mix of germs and allergies, as well as right after the holiday season with all its sugar and booze. This salad is just the meal to set things straight. It's packed with vitamins and minerals, but it's far from boring, with tart green apple, toasted coconut, cashews, avocado, hearty grains, and loads of kale. A tangy lime vinaigrette ties everything together.

It's the Popeye of salads, guaranteed to pick you up and get you going. The crispy chickpeas on page 61 would be a delicious addition.

SERVES 2–4 | PREP TIME: 15 minutes

MAKE THE VINAIGRETTE

1 Combine the lime juice, shallot, and garlic in a small bowl or jar. Season with salt and pepper to taste. Let sit for 5 minutes to allow the flavors to meld. Whisk or shake in the oil.

BUILD THE BOWLS

2 Place the kale in a large bowl and season with salt and pepper. Pour in half of the vinaigrette. Using your hands, massage the kale until slightly softened and dark green, 1 to 2 minutes. Add the grains, apple, cashews, and coconut. Drizzle in more dressing and season with more salt and pepper. Toss to coat. Taste and add more dressing as needed. Top the salad with the avocado slices.

VINAIGRETTE

- 3 tablespoons lime juice
- 1 tablespoon minced shallot
- 1 garlic clove, minced or grated on a Microplane
  Salt and freshly ground black pepper
- ¼ cup extra-virgin olive oil

BOWLS

- 6 cups finely chopped curly kale leaves, stems discarded
  Salt and freshly ground black pepper
- 2 cups cooked grains (cooled)
- ½ green apple, cored and finely chopped
- ⅓ cup toasted cashews, coarsely chopped
- ½ cup toasted unsweetened coconut flakes
- 1 avocado, pitted, peeled, and thinly sliced

MAKE-AHEAD OPTION

The vinaigrette can be refrigerated for up to 5 days.

Other Sauces to Try
- Spicy Lime Dressing (page 123)

QUICK & EASY THAI-STYLE VEGETABLE CURRY

CURRY

- 2 tablespoons virgin coconut oil or neutral vegetable oil (such as grapeseed)
- 2 tablespoons Thai red curry paste
- 1 tablespoon minced fresh gingerroot
- 2 garlic cloves, minced
- 2 cups diced sweet potato
- 2 cups diced eggplant
- 2 cups broccoli florets
- 1 cup coarsely chopped green beans
- 2 (14-ounce) cans coconut milk
- 2–3 teaspoons fish sauce, or as desired (I use 3 teaspoons of Red Boat brand, which is milder than others)
- 1 tablespoon low-sodium tamari or soy sauce
- 1 tablespoon coconut sugar or packed brown sugar
- 1 tablespoon lime juice, plus lime wedges for serving
- Salt

BOWLS

- 1 batch cooked quinoa or rice
- Toasted cashews, for serving
- Chopped fresh basil, mint, and/or cilantro, for serving

Forget takeout. This vegetable-packed, Thai-inspired red curry is healthy, quick, and pretty darn beautiful to boot. I call it my Thursday-night curry, as it's a great way to use up odds and ends lingering in the vegetable drawer at the end of the week. This version uses sweet potato, eggplant, broccoli, and green beans, but butternut squash, cauliflower, bell peppers, zucchini, and kale are all great options. They get simmered in a red curry coconut broth with tamari, fish sauce, lime juice, and fresh herbs.

It's vibrant and sunny, yet warm and comforting, making it perfect for any time of the year. Be sure to prep all your vegetables before beginning, as the process goes fast! I prefer to serve this over rice or quinoa.

SERVES 4 | PREP TIME: 15 minutes | COOKING TIME: 15 minutes

MAKE THE CURRY

1 Heat the oil over medium heat in a large wok or pot. Add the curry paste, gingerroot, and garlic. Cook, stirring, for 1 minute. Add the sweet potato, eggplant, broccoli, and green beans, and toss to coat. Stir in the coconut milk and fish sauce to taste, along with the tamari and sugar. Bring to a boil, then reduce the heat to a simmer. Cook, stirring occasionally, until the vegetables are tender, about 10 minutes. Remove the pot from the heat and stir in the lime juice. Season with salt to taste.

BUILD THE BOWLS

2 Spoon the grains into bowls and spoon the curry over the top. Sprinkle with toasted cashews and basil, and serve with lime wedges.

FISH SAUCE

When it comes to fish sauce, not all brands are created equal. Some are much saltier and fishier than others, and they can end up dominating a dish. I highly recommend Red Boat brand, which is more delicate than others and has a pleasant aroma. You can find it online or at specialty grocery stores.

ROASTED BEETS, CARROTS & CAULIFLOWER
WITH SPINACH + PICK-YOUR-OWN-SAUCE

My favorite way to eat vegetables, hands-down, is roasted: the sweet, caramelized edges and crispy bitter bits are like an addiction. I love the combination of nutty roasted cauliflower, sweet carrots, and earthy beets, but you can use any mix of hearty vegetables. I roast the beets on their own baking sheet so that they don't dye the other vegetables red.

You can serve the roasted veggies, drizzled with the sauce of your choice, with the garlicky spinach salad on the side, or omit the sauce altogether and just mix up a big salad (add a bit more lemon juice and olive oil if you do). This super-healthy meal takes me to crave-me-want-me-need-me territory. I hope you'll join me there.

SERVES 4 | PREP TIME: 10 minutes | COOKING TIME: 35 minutes

MAKE THE VEGGIES

1 Preheat the oven to 425°F (220°C). Line two baking sheets with aluminum foil. Place the beets on one of the baking sheets and drizzle with 1 tablespoon of the oil. Season with salt and pepper, and toss to coat. Spread in an even layer.

2 Place the carrots and cauliflower on the second baking sheet and drizzle with 2 tablespoons of the oil. Season with salt and pepper, and toss to coat. Spread in an even layer.

3 Transfer both pans to the oven and roast, stirring the vegetables and switching the pan positions once or twice during cooking for about 35 minutes, until the vegetables are tender and browned.

4 Combine the lemon juice and garlic in a large bowl. Whisk in the remaining 1 tablespoon oil. Season with salt and pepper to taste. Add the spinach and toss to coat.

BUILD THE BOWLS

5 Spoon the grains into bowls. Arrange the spinach and roasted vegetables over each. Drizzle with the sauce of your choice and sprinkle with the sunflower seeds and chives, if using.

MAKE-AHEAD OPTION

The roasted vegetables can be refrigerated for up to 5 days. Bring to room temperature or reheat slightly before serving.

ROASTED VEGGIES

- 3 medium beets, peeled and cut into ½-inch dice
- 4 tablespoons extra-virgin olive oil

  Salt and freshly ground black pepper
- 2 medium carrots, trimmed and sliced ¼ inch thick
- 1 small head cauliflower, cored and cut into small florets
- 1 tablespoon lemon juice
- 1 small garlic clove, grated on a Microplane
- 3 cups baby spinach

BOWLS

- 1 batch cooked grains

  CHOICE OF
  - Tahini Sauce (page 94)
  - Coconut-Peanut Sauce (page 119)
  - Mint & Cilantro Sauce (page 146)
  - Smoky Red Pepper Sauce (page 61)
  - Classic Pesto (page 79)
  - Mint Pesto (page 65)

  Toasted sunflower seeds (or toasted nuts of your choice), for serving

  Sliced fresh chives, for serving (optional)

ROASTED BUTTERNUT SQUASH, APPLE & GOAT CHEESE SALAD

1 (2-pound) butternut squash, peeled and cut into ½-inch dice (4 cups)

6 garlic cloves (unpeeled)

2 teaspoons minced fresh sage

2 teaspoons balsamic vinegar

¼ cup plus 1½ tablespoons extra-virgin olive oil

Salt and freshly ground black pepper

¾ cup pecans

1 tablespoon plus 1½ teaspoons maple syrup

2 tablespoons apple cider vinegar

BOWLS

1 batch cooked sorghum, brown rice, wheat berries, spelt berries, Khorasan wheat (Kamut), farro, or einkorn (cooled)

1 crisp apple (such as Fuji, Pink Lady, or Granny Smith), cored and cut into ½-inch dice

2–4 ounces goat cheese, crumbled

Fried sage leaves, for serving (see opposite page, optional)

MAKE-AHEAD OPTIONS

Store the maple pecans at room temperature or in the refrigerator for up to 1 week.

Refrigerate the dressing for up to 5 days.

When I entertain, I plan menus that can be made almost entirely in advance. That way, I can enjoy the company of my guests without being tethered to the stove or sink. This is one of my favorite make-ahead salads, and it's especially beautiful on a Thanksgiving buffet. Caramelized butternut squash is tossed with maple-roasted pecans, chewy grains, crisp apples, goat cheese, and a roasted garlic dressing. It's savory, sweet, and full of texture.

The salad can happily sit at room temperature for several hours. If you want to really gussy it up, garnish it with fried sage leaves just before serving.

For a vegan variation, omit the cheese.

SERVES 6 | PREP TIME: 20 minutes | COOKING TIME: 30 minutes

1 Preheat the oven to 400°F (200°C). Line one baking sheet with aluminum foil and another baking sheet with parchment paper.

2 Place the butternut squash, garlic, and 1½ teaspoons of the minced sage on the foil-lined baking sheet. Drizzle with the balsamic vinegar and 1½ tablespoons of the oil. Season with salt and pepper, and toss to coat. Roast the squash, stirring occasionally, for about 30 minutes, or until tender and caramelized around the edges. Taste and season with additional salt and pepper, if needed.

3 While the squash cooks, make the maple pecans. Dump the pecans onto the parchment-lined baking sheet and drizzle with 1 tablespoon of the maple syrup. Season with salt to taste. Toss well to coat, then spread the nuts in a single layer. Bake for 5 to 7 minutes, until the nuts are a shade darker in color and aromatic. Sprinkle with a bit more salt and let cool (the nuts will harden as they cool). Coarsely chop.

4 To make the dressing, squeeze the roasted garlic cloves out of their skins into a small bowl and mash them into a paste with a pinch of salt. Add the apple cider vinegar, the remaining 1½ teaspoons maple syrup, and the remaining ½ teaspoon minced sage. Whisk in the remaining ¼ cup oil. Season with salt and pepper to taste.

5 Combine the butternut squash, cooked grains, apple, and chopped maple pecans in a large bowl. Add the dressing and toss to coat. Taste and season with salt and pepper as needed. Gently fold in the goat cheese. If you're feeling fancy, top with fried sage leaves just before serving.

CRISPY FRIED SAGE LEAVES

When lightly fried, sage leaves turn mild and delightfully crisp. You can eat them on their own or use them as a garnish. To fry sage leaves, heat ¼ inch of vegetable oil in a small skillet over medium heat until shimmering. Carefully add sage leaves in a single layer, being careful not to overcrowd the pan (they should start to bubble immediately). Cook until the leaves start to crisp up and darken but not brown, flipping once, about 30 seconds total. Transfer to paper towels to drain and season with salt to taste. Store at room temperature, uncovered, for up to 3 hours.

BUDDHA BOWLS WITH CRISPY CHICKPEAS + HUMMUS, PAGE 101

⑥
LEGUMES

D
on't turn the page! While I know that beans might not be the sexiest of foods, I promise you that these recipes are some of the most seductive in the book. As an inexpensive and nutritious source of protein and fiber, canned beans and quick-cooking lentils are the foundations for a zillion weeknight meals in my house, including the dishes on the following pages.

Beans are especially perfect for showcasing robust spices and sauces, from an Indian–inspired dal that's pure comfort in a bowl to a pan-fried falafel that's easy enough for a Wednesday, and from the easiest soup you'll ever make (with a garlicky pesto you'll want to spoon over everything) to a cumin-scented black rice and white bean salad that's stylish enough for a runway. These aren't mere bean recipes, people: they're ravishing *legumes*.

PANFRIED FALAFEL
WITH CUCUMBER, TOMATOES, OLIVES & ROMAINE
+ TAHINI SAUCE

TAHINI SAUCE

- 1 garlic clove, peeled
- ½ cup well-stirred tahini
- 2 tablespoons lemon juice
  Salt
- ¼ cup plus 2 tablespoons water

MAKE-AHEAD OPTIONS

The tahini sauce can sit, covered, at room temperature for up to 6 hours, or it can be refrigerated for up to 5 days. Bring to room temperature before serving (if needed, thin it with another 1 to 2 tablespoons of water).

The shaped falafel can be covered tightly with plastic wrap and refrigerated overnight.

Other Sauces to Try

- Garlic Yogurt (page 99)
- Minty Yogurt (page 158)
- Hummus (page 101)

Homemade falafel on a weeknight? In less than an hour? Yes, you can! These are the easiest falafel ever, made with canned chickpeas and a heap of fresh herbs right in the food processor. The falafel patties are panfried until golden and crisp and are served over quinoa with grape tomatoes, cucumber, black olives, and a zippy romaine salad. A velvety, dairy-free tahini sauce ties everything together.

You can make the falafel with either oat or almond flour — oat flour creates slightly denser falafel patties that are easier to flip, while the almond flour falafel are a bit lighter but crumblier in texture.

SERVES 4 | PREP TIME: 40 minutes | COOKING TIME: 10 minutes

MAKE THE SAUCE

1 Drop the garlic clove into a food processor with the blade running. Add the tahini and lemon juice, and season with salt. Process until smooth, scraping down the sides as needed. With the blade running, slowly pour the water through the feed tube. Scrape the sides and bottom of the work bowl and process again until the mixture is light and creamy. Season with salt to taste.

MAKE THE FALAFEL

2 Line a baking sheet with parchment paper. Drop the garlic cloves into a food processor with the blade running. Add the parsley, cilantro, and scallion. Process until the herbs are finely chopped. Add the chickpeas, cumin, lemon juice, and tahini. Season with salt and pepper to taste. Pulse until the chickpeas are finely chopped and sticky, about 20 pulses — you should still see little chickpea chunks (you're not going for a purée).

3 Transfer the mixture to a bowl and gently fold in the flour. Season with salt and pepper to taste. Form the mixture into 12 patties (they should be about 2 inches wide and ½ inch thick). Place the patties on the parchment-lined baking sheet.

4 Heat 3 tablespoons of the vegetable oil in a large nonstick or cast-iron skillet over medium-high heat. Arrange half of the falafel in the pan, leaving plenty of space in between each. Cook until golden brown on the bottom, about 2 minutes. Flip and cook until golden on the other side, 1 to 2 minutes longer. Transfer to paper towels and season with salt. Pour in another 1 to 2 tablespoons of oil (as needed) and repeat with the remaining falafel.

BUILD THE BOWLS

5 Toss the romaine and red onion, if using, with the lemon juice and olive oil in a large bowl. Season with salt and pepper.

6 Spoon the grains into bowls. Arrange the falafel, tomatoes, cucumber, and olives over each bowl. Drizzle with the tahini sauce and top with the romaine salad. Sprinkle with a few parsley and/or cilantro leaves.

HOMEMADE OAT AND ALMOND FLOURS

If you don't have oat or almond flour on hand, you can make your own from scratch. Simply place old-fashioned rolled oats or raw almonds (no more than 1 cup) in a food processor or high-speed blender (such as a Vitamix) and pulse until very finely ground (be careful not to overprocess the almonds, or you'll end up with almond butter). Store the flour in an airtight container at room temperature for 1 week, or refrigerate it for up to 1 month.

FALAFEL

3 garlic cloves, peeled

1 cup lightly packed fresh flat-leaf parsley, plus more for serving

1 cup lightly packed fresh cilantro, plus more for serving

1 scallion, coarsely chopped

1 (15-ounce) can chickpeas, drained, rinsed, and patted dry with paper towels

1 teaspoon ground cumin

2 tablespoons lemon juice

1 tablespoon tahini

Salt and freshly ground black pepper

2 tablespoons oat or almond flour

4–6 tablespoons neutral vegetable oil (such as grapeseed)

BOWLS

1½ cups thinly sliced romaine lettuce

½ small red onion, very thinly sliced and rinsed in cold water (optional)

1 tablespoon lemon juice

1 teaspoon extra-virgin olive oil

1 batch cooked quinoa, black rice, or millet

1½ cups cherry or grape tomatoes, halved

½ English cucumber, sliced

½ cup kalamata olives

Parsley and/or cilantro leaves

BLACK (RICE) & WHITE (BEAN) SALAD
+ CUMIN VINAIGRETTE

This salad is a real looker, but it's much more than a pretty face. With white beans, arugula, shaved carrots, raisins, walnuts, and feta, along with a spicy cumin vinaigrette, this one's got brawn *and* brains. Cumin is a natural partner for both beans and carrots (in fact, it's in the same family as carrots, botanically speaking), and here it lends its slightly smoky, herbal flavor to a quick vinaigrette that also features turmeric and cinnamon for warmth.

Rinsing the shallot in cold water before adding it to the salad helps remove some of its bite. If you happen to have any cilantro and/or mint lying around, they're both delicious additions to the salad.

For a vegan variation, omit the cheese.

SERVES 4–6 | PREP TIME: 15 minutes

MAKE THE VINAIGRETTE

1 Place the vinegar, oil, maple syrup, mustard, cumin, turmeric, cinnamon, and cayenne in a bowl or jar. Whisk or shake to combine. Season with salt and black pepper to taste.

BUILD THE BOWLS

2 Combine the rice, beans, shallot, arugula, carrot, raisins, walnuts, and feta in a large bowl. Season with salt and black pepper to taste. Drizzle with vinaigrette (you might not need it all) and toss to combine. Serve with additional feta sprinkled over the top.

MAKE-AHEAD OPTION

The vinaigrette can be refrigerated for up to 5 days.

VINAIGRETTE

- ¼ cup apple cider vinegar
- ⅓ cup extra-virgin olive oil
- 1 tablespoon maple syrup
- 1 tablespoon grainy mustard
- 1 teaspoon ground cumin
- ½ teaspoon ground turmeric
- ¼ teaspoon ground cinnamon
- ⅛ teaspoon cayenne pepper

  Salt and freshly ground black pepper

BOWLS

- 1 batch cooked black rice (cooled)
- 1 (15-ounce) can white beans (such as cannellini or navy), rinsed and drained
- 1 small shallot, minced and rinsed in cold water
- 3 cups (or 3 big handfuls) baby arugula, baby kale, or baby spinach
- 1 medium carrot, shaved with a vegetable peeler
- ¾ cup golden raisins
- ½ cup coarsely chopped toasted walnuts
- ½ cup crumbled feta cheese, plus more for serving

  Salt and freshly ground black pepper

MARINATED BEAN SALAD
WITH ROASTED RED PEPPERS & CUCUMBERS

MARINATED BEANS

- ¼ cup champagne vinegar or white wine vinegar
- 1 small shallot, minced (about 3 tablespoons)
- 1 large garlic clove, minced

  Salt and freshly ground black pepper
- ½ cup finely chopped fresh herbs, such as parsley, dill, mint, and/or chives (preferably a mix)
- ⅛ teaspoon red pepper flakes
- ½ cup extra-virgin olive oil
- 2 (15-ounce) cans beans (such as navy, cannellini, chickpeas, and/or black-eyed peas), rinsed and drained

BOWLS

- 1 batch cooked sorghum, wheat berries, spelt berries, Khorasan wheat (Kamut), farro, einkorn, or barley (cooled)
- ½ cup diced roasted red bell pepper
- 1 cup finely diced English cucumber (about ½ small cucumber)

  Crumbled goat or feta cheese, for serving (optional)

This salad is chewy, crunchy, and herby, and it only gets better with age (like most things in life, right?). Hearty grains, such as sorghum, wheat, or barley, hold up well in a bright vinaigrette that's packed with fresh herbs. A mix of beans (nearly any variety will work) provides substance, while roasted red peppers and cucumbers bring sweetness and crunch.

This salad is highly adaptable — feel free to toss in a few handfuls of spinach or arugula, some chopped nuts, shaved cheese, or hard-boiled eggs. It's one of my very favorite dishes to pack for picnics and potlucks.

For a vegan variation, omit the cheese.

SERVES 4 | PREP TIME: 15 minutes

MAKE THE BEANS

1 Place the vinegar in a large bowl and add the shallot and garlic. Season with salt and black pepper. Let sit for 5 to 10 minutes to infuse. Add the herbs, pepper flakes, and oil. Whisk to combine. Fold in the beans.

BUILD THE BOWLS

2 Add the grains, roasted red peppers, and cucumbers to the bowl. Season with salt and black pepper to taste, and toss well to combine. Divide into serving bowls. If you'd like, sprinkle with crumbled goat cheese before serving.

MARINATED BEANS

The marinated beans are fantastic in their own right. I love having a stash of them in my fridge, which I not only toss into salads like this one but also spoon over crostini for a quick lunch or appetizer. Store covered for up to 1 week.

MUJADARRA
WITH CARAMELIZED ONIONS & WALNUTS + GARLIC YOGURT

Mujadarra is a Middle Eastern dish of lentils, rice, and fried onions that's served with yogurt. Like some of the tastiest foods on earth, it proves that simple is often best.

This version incorporates spinach (which isn't traditional but is a great way to sneak in added nutrition). Served with meltingly soft caramelized onions, a quick garlic yogurt, and chopped walnuts for texture, it's proof that humble food can be oh-so-fine indeed. While it makes for a great meal on its own, this is also fantastic with the lamb kofte on page 144.

For a vegan variation, omit the garlic yogurt.

SERVES 4 | **PREP TIME:** 15 minutes | **COOKING TIME:** 30 minutes

MAKE THE GARLIC YOGURT

1 Combine the lemon juice and grated garlic in a small bowl. Let sit for 5 minutes (this will mellow out the garlic). Stir in the yogurt and season with salt and pepper.

BUILD THE BOWLS

2 Heat the ghee in a large skillet over medium heat. Add the onion and cumin seeds and season with salt and pepper. Cook, stirring occasionally, until the onions are dark golden and soft, adjusting the heat and adding a few splashes of water as needed during the cooking process to prevent burning, 20 to 25 minutes.

3 Place the lentils in a medium pot with the water, garlic clove, parsley sprig, and bay leaf. Bring to a boil, then reduce the heat to a simmer and cook until tender but not mushy (they should still have a slight bite), 15 to 20 minutes. Drain and transfer the lentils back to the pot. Remove the garlic, bay leaf, and parsley sprig and discard.

4 Stir the rice into the lentils, along with the spinach and broth. Season with salt and pepper to taste. Cook over medium heat, stirring often, until warmed through. Stir in the chopped parsley.

5 Spoon the mujadarra into bowls and top with the caramelized onions. Dollop with the garlic yogurt and sprinkle with chopped walnuts. Serve with lemon wedges.

Other Sauces to Try
- Minty Yogurt (page 158)

GARLIC YOGURT

2 teaspoons lemon juice

1 garlic clove, grated on a Microplane

1 (7-ounce) container (¾ cup) Greek yogurt (preferably 2% or whole-milk)

Salt and freshly ground black pepper

BOWLS

2 tablespoons ghee or extra-virgin olive oil

1 large onion, thinly sliced

¼ teaspoon cumin seeds

Salt and freshly ground black pepper

1 cup brown or green lentils, rinsed and drained

2 cups water

1 garlic clove, smashed

1 fresh flat-leaf parsley sprig plus 1 tablespoon chopped leaves

1 bay leaf

1 batch cooked brown or white rice

½ cup finely chopped spinach

¼ cup low-sodium vegetable or chicken broth

Chopped toasted walnuts, for serving

Lemon wedges, for serving

BUDDHA BOWLS
WITH CRISPY CHICKPEAS + HUMMUS

A Buddha bowl is a hearty bowl of healthy vegetables, grains, and lean protein, packed so full that it resembles the rounded belly of the Buddha. Making and eating these delicious creations will make you feel as balanced as the Buddha himself. Most of the recipes in this book fit the Buddha bowl description, but this is a classic iteration, featuring roasted sweet potatoes and crispy za'atar chickpeas, along with carrots, beets, avocado, and a quick homemade hummus. Feel free to replace the hummus with just about any other sauce.

SERVES 4 | **PREP TIME:** 15 minutes | **COOKING TIME:** 30 minutes

MAKE THE HUMMUS

1 Drain the chickpeas, reserving 3 tablespoons of the liquid. Rinse the chickpeas well and shake dry. Drop the garlic clove into a food processor with the blade running. Add the chickpeas, tahini, lemon juice, and the reserved chickpea liquid. Season with salt to taste. Process until smooth, scraping the sides occasionally. With the blade running, slowly drizzle the oil through the feed tube. Process until combined. If you prefer a looser consistency, pulse in a splash of water. Taste and season with additional salt, if needed.

BUILD THE BOWLS

2 Preheat the oven to 400°F (200°C). Line two baking sheets with aluminum foil.

3 Place the sweet potato on one of the baking sheets and drizzle with 1 tablespoon of the oil. Season with salt and pepper and toss to coat. Spread in a single layer.

4 Pat the chickpeas dry using paper towels. Transfer them to the second baking sheet and drizzle with the remaining 1 tablespoon of oil. Sprinkle with the za'atar and season with salt and pepper. Toss to coat.

5 Roast the sweet potatoes and chickpeas for 15 minutes. Stir both (flip the potatoes if they are cut into wedges). Continue roasting for 10 to 15 minutes longer, until the potatoes are tender and the chickpeas are golden brown and starting to split.

6 Spoon the grains into bowls. Arrange the sweet potatoes, chickpeas, beets, carrots, cucumber, avocado, and hummus on top. Drizzle with a bit of oil and sprinkle with hemp seeds, along with a bit more za'atar, if using. Serve with lemon wedges.

HUMMUS

- 1 (15-ounce) can chickpeas
- 1 small garlic clove, peeled
- 2 tablespoons tahini
- 2 tablespoons lemon juice
- Salt
- 2 tablespoons extra-virgin olive oil

BOWLS

- 1 large sweet potato, diced or cut into ½-inch wedges
- 2 tablespoons olive oil, plus more for serving
- Salt and freshly ground black pepper
- 1 (15-ounce) can chickpeas, rinsed and drained
- 1 teaspoon za'atar, plus more for serving (optional)
- 1 batch cooked grains
- 1 large beet, shredded or spiralized
- 2 medium carrots, shredded, shaved, or spiralized
- ½ English cucumber, sliced
- 1 avocado, pitted, peeled, and diced
- Hemp seeds or sesame seeds, for serving
- Lemon wedges, for serving

SPICE SUB

If you don't have za'atar, you can season the chickpeas with a range of other spices: chili powder, cumin, garlic powder, and/or paprika are all good bets.

EASIEST-EVER WHITE BEAN SOUP
+ SUN-DRIED TOMATO PESTO

PESTO

- 2 garlic cloves, peeled
- 1 (10-ounce) jar sun-dried tomatoes in olive oil
- ⅓ cup lightly packed fresh basil leaves
- ⅓ cup grated Parmesan cheese
- 1 teaspoon lemon juice

  Salt and freshly ground black pepper

SOUP

- 6 cups low-sodium vegetable or chicken broth
- 1 (2-inch) Parmigiano-Reggiano cheese rind, plus shaved Parmesan for serving
- 1 (15-ounce) can cannellini beans, rinsed and drained
- 2 cups cooked quinoa, sorghum, brown rice, wheat berries, spelt berries, Khorasan wheat (Kamut), farro, einkorn, or barley
- 1 cup frozen peas
- 5 ounces baby spinach
- 2 tablespoons lemon juice

  Salt and freshly ground black pepper

  Torn fresh basil leaves, for serving (optional)

Other Sauces to Try
- Classic Pesto (page 79)
- Salsa Verde (page 150)

For those nights when you're craving something nourishing and restorative but can't bear to even pull out a knife, this soup comes to your rescue. I was inspired by a sun-dried tomato broth recipe that I ripped out of *Food & Wine* years ago, which became one of my favorite hacks for speedy soups.

The secret is in infusing store-bought vegetable or chicken broth with two powerhouse ingredients: a Parmigiano-Reggiano cheese rind, which adds nutty complexity; and a quick sun-dried tomato pesto, which lends sparkling richness. I use cannellini beans and grains for substance, along with frozen peas and baby spinach for color and flavor (no chopping necessary!).

For the pesto, be sure to use a 10-ounce jar (net weight) of sun-dried tomatoes. Some brands, such as Mediterranean Organic, list the *direct weight* as 5 ounces on the label, but using two jars will yield totally different results — for that brand, use a little more than one jar.

SERVES 4　|　PREP TIME: 5 minutes　|　COOKING TIME: 25 minutes

MAKE THE PESTO

1 Drop the garlic clove into a food processor with the blade running. Add the sun-dried tomatoes with their oil and process until coarsely chopped. Add the basil, Parmesan, and lemon juice, and process until smooth. Season with salt and pepper to taste.

MAKE THE SOUP

2 Bring the broth and Parmesan rind to a boil in a medium pot, stirring occasionally to prevent the rind from sticking to the bottom. Reduce the heat to a simmer and let cook for 5 minutes.

3 Add the cannellini beans and grains, and simmer for 5 to 10 minutes longer. Stir in the peas and spinach, and cook until the spinach is wilted (it will look like a ton of spinach, but it will cook down!). Remove the pot from the heat and stir in ⅓ cup of the pesto and the lemon juice. Season generously with salt and pepper (you'll need more than you think, especially if your broth was unsalted).

4 Ladle the soup into bowls and top with a big dollop of the pesto (this is key for flavor!). Sprinkle with shaved Parmesan and torn basil leaves, if using.

CUCUMBER TABBOULEH
WITH CHICKPEAS & FETA

When we have guests over, I love to set out a big meze platter of tabbouleh, hummus, marinated feta, and cucumber slices as an appetizer. One day I decided to simply combine all of those flavors into one dish. The result was a gorgeous salad packed with parsley and mint, as well as buttery chickpeas, crisp cucumbers, juicy tomatoes, and salty feta.

Instead of using the traditional bulgur wheat, I make the tabbouleh with millet or quinoa, meaning this version is also gluten-free. It's fabulous on its own or as a side dish to lamb, fish, or chicken.

For a vegan variation, omit the cheese.

SERVES 4–6 | **PREP TIME:** 15 minutes

1 Cut off and discard the tough bottom stems of the parsley (1 to 2 inches). Finely chop the rest of the stems and leaves (you should have about 1 heaping cup).

2 Place the chopped parsley in a large bowl and add the scallions, chickpeas, cucumber, tomatoes, mint, and garlic. Fold in the quinoa, cumin, lemon juice, and oil. Season with salt and pepper to taste. Sprinkle the feta over the top.

1 bunch fresh flat-leaf parsley

2 scallions, finely chopped

1 (15-ounce) can chickpeas, rinsed and drained

1 cup finely diced English cucumber (about ½ medium cucumber)

1 cup finely diced seeded tomatoes or halved grape tomatoes

¼ cup finely chopped fresh mint

2 garlic cloves, minced

2 cups cooked quinoa or millet (cooled)

1 teaspoon ground cumin

3 tablespoons lemon juice

3 tablespoons extra-virgin olive oil

Salt and freshly ground black pepper

½ cup crumbled feta cheese

MAKE-AHEAD OPTION

The tabbouleh can be stored at room temperature for up to 2 hours, or refrigerated for up to 1 day.

CURRIED RED LENTIL & SWEET POTATO DAL WITH KALE & TOASTED COCONUT

Dal is one of the easiest, least expensive, and most satisfying foods on this planet. It's an Indian dish of simmered lentils, peas, or beans, and it's perfect for fast weeknight dinners. This version uses quick-cooking red lentils with coconut milk, curry powder, and sweet potatoes, which aren't traditional but which provide sweetness. I pair it with quickly sautéed kale (you can use any leafy green), as well as toasted cashews and coconut flakes.

You can buy toasted coconut flakes or you can toast them yourself in a 325°F (170°C) oven for 5 to 10 minutes (keep a close eye on them and stir often, as they go from golden to blackened quickly). I prefer quinoa, millet, or rice for these bowls. The dal is also delicious with naan bread.

SERVES 4 | **PREP TIME:** 15 minutes | **COOKING TIME:** 30 minutes

MAKE THE DAL

1 Heat the oil in a large pot over medium heat. Add the onion and season with salt and pepper. Cook, stirring occasionally, until tender, 3 to 4 minutes. Add the sweet potato and cook, stirring occasionally, until the onion is golden, about 2 minutes longer.

2 Add the garlic, gingerroot, curry powder, and lentils, and cook, stirring, until fragrant, 1 to 2 minutes. Pour in the broth and coconut milk and add the cilantro sprigs. Bring to a boil, then reduce the heat to a simmer. Cook, stirring occasionally, until the lentils and sweet potatoes are soft and the mixture is thickened but still soupy, about 20 minutes. Stir in the lime juice and season with salt and pepper to taste.

BUILD THE BOWLS

3 Heat the oil in a large skillet over medium heat. Add the kale, and season with salt and pepper. Drizzle in the water. Cover and cook, stirring occasionally, until wilted and tender, 3 to 5 minutes. Stir in the lime juice.

4 Spoon the grains into bowls and top with the dal and greens. Sprinkle with toasted coconut, cashews, and cilantro leaves. Serve with mango chutney and lime wedges.

MAKE-AHEAD OPTION

Refrigerate the dal for up to 5 days. Reheat before serving, thinning with a few splashes of water as needed.

DAL

- 2 tablespoons virgin coconut oil
- 1 medium onion, finely diced
- Salt and freshly ground black pepper
- ½ medium sweet potato, peeled and finely diced
- 2 garlic cloves, minced
- 2 teaspoons minced fresh gingerroot
- 2 teaspoons curry powder
- 1 cup red lentils, rinsed and drained
- 2 cups low-sodium vegetable or chicken broth
- 1 (14-ounce) can coconut milk
- 2 fresh cilantro sprigs
- 1 teaspoon lime juice

BOWLS

- 1 tablespoon virgin coconut oil
- ½ bunch kale, stems discarded, leaves coarsely chopped (about 4 cups chopped)
- 2 tablespoons water
- 1 tablespoon lime juice
- 1 batch cooked quinoa, millet, or rice

TOPPINGS

- Toasted unsweetened coconut flakes
- Chopped toasted cashews
- Cilantro leaves
- Mango chutney
- Lime wedges

ROASTED CAULIFLOWER & SQUASH
WITH BLACK BEANS & AVOCADO + CREAMY CHIPOTLE SAUCE

SAUCE

- 1 garlic clove, peeled
- ⅔ cup Greek yogurt
- 2 tablespoons mayonnaise
- 1 tablespoon lime juice
- 1 tablespoon water
- 2 teaspoons honey
- 1 teaspoon extra-virgin olive oil
- 1–2 teaspoons adobo sauce (from a can of chipotle chiles in adobo)
- Salt and freshly ground black pepper

BOWLS

- 1 medium Delicata squash
- 2 teaspoons maple syrup
- 2 tablespoons plus 1 teaspoon extra-virgin olive oil
- ½ teaspoon chili powder
- Salt and freshly ground black pepper
- 1 small head cauliflower, cut into 1-inch florets
- ½ teaspoon ground cumin
- 1 (15-ounce) can black beans, rinsed and drained
- 1 small garlic clove, grated on a Microplane
- Juice of 1 lime
- 1 batch cooked quinoa, rice, or millet

TOPPINGS

- 1 avocado, pitted, peeled, and sliced
- Toasted pepitas
- Fresh cilantro leaves

With roasted Delicata squash, caramelized cauliflower, garlicky black beans, and a creamy chipotle sauce, this dish is both crave-worthy *and* comforting. This is one of my very favorite sauces, and you're going to want to eat it on everything — try drizzling it over tacos, salads, or the Crispy Fish Taco Bowls on page 154.

SERVES 4 | PREP TIME: 20 minutes | COOKING TIME: 25 minutes

MAKE THE SAUCE

1 Place the garlic clove in a mini food processor and process until coarsely chopped. Add the yogurt, mayonnaise, lime juice, water, honey, oil, and 1 teaspoon of the adobo. Season with salt and pepper. Process until smooth. Taste and add another teaspoon of the adobo sauce, if you prefer a spicier sauce.

BUILD THE BOWLS

2 Preheat the oven to 425°F (220°C). Line two baking sheets with aluminum foil.

3 Trim off the ends of the squash, then cut the squash in half lengthwise. Scrape out and discard the seeds. Slice each half crosswise into ½-inch-thick slices. Place the squash in a large bowl and drizzle with the maple syrup and 1 tablespoon of the oil. Sprinkle with the chili powder and season with salt and pepper. Toss well to coat. Spread the squash out in a single layer on one of the baking sheets.

4 Place the cauliflower in the same bowl (no need to wash it) and drizzle with 1 tablespoon of the oil. Sprinkle with the cumin and season with salt and pepper. Toss well to coat. Spread the cauliflower out on the second baking sheet in a single layer.

5 Roast the vegetables for about 25 minutes, or until caramelized and tender, flipping over the squash slices and stirring the cauliflower halfway through.

6 While the vegetables roast, toss the black beans with the grated garlic, lime juice, and the remaining 1 teaspoon oil. Season with salt and pepper to taste.

7 Spoon the grains into bowls. Arrange the roasted squash, cauliflower, and black beans over the top. Drizzle with the sauce and top with the avocado slices, pepitas, and cilantro leaves.

Other Sauces to Try
- Guacamole (page 115)

SOUTHWESTERN PINTO BEANS
WITH SWISS CHARD & AVOCADO
+ ROASTED RED PEPPER & CASHEW SAUCE

ROASTED RED PEPPER & CASHEW SAUCE

½ cup cashews

1 large red bell pepper, halved lengthwise, core and seeds discarded

2 large garlic cloves (unpeeled)

½ cup water

2 tablespoons apple cider vinegar

¼ teaspoon sugar

⅛ teaspoon cayenne pepper

Salt and freshly ground black pepper

MAKE-AHEAD OPTION

The sauce can be refrigerated for up to 5 days. Serve warm or at room temperature.

Other Sauces to Try

- Creamy Chipotle Sauce (page 106)
- Guacamole (page 115)
- Avocado, Corn & Tomato Relish (page 134)

While we can never count on a huge tomato or cucumber harvest in our backyard garden (thanks to a family of cunning little chipmunks), we can always rely on an epic output of Swiss chard. It grows from early spring to late fall, and I use it in tarts, pastas, tacos, and grain bowls. Here you sauté it with red onion and garlic, and pair it with smoky bacon-flecked pinto beans and a silky red pepper sauce.

The sauce is slightly sweet and spicy and is thickened with soaked cashews, which lend a rich texture (you've got to try it with the Grilled Skirt Steak with Sweet Corn & Cabbage Slaw on page 141). With salty cheese, buttery avocado, and pepitas, this bowl hits all the right notes (and it's also delicious in taco form). If you're able to make the sauce ahead of time, the bowls come together really quickly.

For a vegan variation, swap out the bacon in the beans for 1 tablespoon olive oil.

SERVES 4 | **PREP TIME:** 30 minutes, plus 4–12 hours to soak the cashews
COOKING TIME: 30 minutes

MAKE THE SAUCE

1 Place the cashews in a small bowl and cover with water. Let sit at room temperature for 4 to 12 hours (or overnight).

2 Preheat the oven to 450°F (230°C). Line a baking sheet with aluminum foil. Place the bell pepper halves on the baking sheet, cut sides down, along with the garlic cloves. Roast for 15 to 20 minutes, until the pepper pieces are lightly blistered. Let cool, then peel off the skins (it's okay if not all the skin comes off). Peel off the garlic skins. Transfer the vegetables to a high-speed blender.

3 Drain the cashews and add them to the blender, along with the water, vinegar, sugar, and cayenne. Blend until smooth. Season with salt and black pepper to taste.

BUILD THE BOWLS

4 Cook the bacon in a large skillet, preferably nonstick, over medium heat, stirring occasionally, until the fat has rendered and the bacon starts to crisp up and brown. Add the chili powder and cumin, and let them sizzle for a few seconds. Pour in the drained pinto beans and season with salt and black pepper. Cook, stirring with a rubber spatula, until the beans are warmed through and slightly crusty, 2 to 3 minutes. Remove the pan from the heat. Squeeze in the juice from one lime half and stir in the chopped cilantro. Transfer to a bowl.

5 In the same skillet (don't wash it — all those brown bits will add flavor!), heat the oil over medium-high heat. Add the onion and season with salt and black pepper. Cook, stirring, until golden and tender, 3 to 4 minutes. Add the garlic and cook, stirring, for 30 seconds. Pile in the Swiss chard and season with a bit more salt and black pepper. Cook, stirring occasionally, until the chard is wilted and tender, 2 to 3 minutes (if the pan starts to look dry, drizzle in a tablespoon or two of water). Remove the pan from the heat and squeeze in the juice from the remaining lime half.

6 Spoon the grains into bowls. Arrange the pinto beans, Swiss chard, and avocado over the top and drizzle with the roasted red pepper and cashew sauce. Sprinkle with pepitas, crumbled cheese (if using), and cilantro leaves.

BOWLS

- 2 thick-cut bacon strips, chopped
- 1 teaspoon chili powder
- ½ teaspoon ground cumin
- 1 (15-ounce) can pinto beans, rinsed and drained
- Salt and freshly ground black pepper
- 1 lime, halved
- 2 tablespoons chopped fresh cilantro, plus leaves for serving
- 2 tablespoons extra-virgin olive oil
- ½ medium red onion, thinly sliced
- 2 garlic cloves, minced
- 1 bunch Swiss chard, thick bottom stems discarded, leaves and upper stems coarsely chopped
- 1 batch cooked grains
- 1 avocado, pitted, peeled, and diced
- Toasted pepitas, for serving
- Crumbled cotija or feta cheese, for serving (optional)

PORK BANH MI BOWLS + SRIRACHA-MAPLE YOGURT, PAGE 126

CHICKEN, TURKEY & PORK

I f Ella and Juniper had to pick a favorite chapter, this would probably be it. These recipes rank up there as some of their favorite dinners, and mine, too. Disregard any notions that lean white meats are bland — with a quick marinade, spice rub, or sauce, chicken, turkey, and pork can be transformed into dazzling dishes that the whole family will love.

From easy Italian and Asian meatballs that are considered staples in our house to a light Thai-inspired turkey fried rice, and from deconstructed banh mi bowls with a creamy maple-sriracha sauce (do I even need to say anything else?) to a Vietnamese chicken salad that we nicknamed the "flavor bomb," these recipes incorporate a veritable world of flavor using ingredients that you might already have on hand or can easily find. They're some of my go-to weeknight staples, and I hope they'll become yours as well.

ASIAN MEATBALLS
WITH SESAME BROCCOLI + SWEET & SPICY GLAZE

SWEET & SPICY GLAZE

- 1 cup low-sodium chicken broth
- 2 tablespoons low-sodium tamari or soy sauce
- 1 tablespoon rice vinegar
- 2 teaspoons toasted sesame oil
- 2 tablespoons honey
- 1 tablespoon plus 1 teaspoon cornstarch
- 1–2 teaspoons sriracha, as desired
- 1 tablespoon neutral vegetable oil (such as grapeseed)
- 2 teaspoons grated fresh gingerroot
- 1 large garlic clove, grated on a Microplane

MAKE-AHEAD OPTIONS

Refrigerate the glaze for up to 5 days. Reheat before adding the meatballs.

Refrigerate uncooked meatballs for up to 1 day. Cooked meatballs can be frozen for up to 2 months. Thaw in the refrigerator.

I've rarely met a homemade meatball I didn't like, and these beauties rank high on my list of favorites, especially since I can throw them together on a weeknight with minimal effort. They're made with ground turkey (dark meat is juicier and more tender than white meat) and flavored with garlic, gingerroot, scallions, and tamari. They cook quickly in a hot oven and are then tossed in an irresistible sweet and spicy glaze, which is a variation on my sauce for sesame chicken (you can find that recipe at fromscratchfast.com).

Serve the meatballs with sesame broccoli, which roasts right alongside them. I recommend starting the meatballs and broccoli, then making the glaze while they cook.

SERVES 4 | PREP TIME: 30 minutes | COOKING TIME: 25 minutes

MAKE THE GLAZE

1 Whisk together the chicken broth, tamari, vinegar, sesame oil, honey, cornstarch, and sriracha (I prefer 2 teaspoons, but I start with 1 teaspoon if I'm feeding kids) in a large bowl.

2 Combine the vegetable oil, gingerroot, and garlic in a saucepan big enough to hold the meatballs as well. Cook over medium heat, stirring, until the mixture is sizzling and fragrant, about 1 minute. Whisk in the sauce mixture and bring to a boil, stirring. Boil, whisking occasionally, until thickened, 2 minutes. Set aside.

BUILD THE BOWLS

3 Preheat the oven to 450°F (230°C) with racks in the lower third and upper third of the oven. Line one baking sheet with parchment paper and one baking sheet with aluminum foil.

4 Combine the turkey, panko, scallion, garlic, gingerroot, 2 teaspoons of the tamari, and the egg in a large bowl. Season with salt and pepper. Mix everything together using a fork. Shape into 1½-inch balls and arrange them in a single layer on the parchment-lined baking sheet.

5 Arrange the broccoli florets on the foil-lined baking sheet and toss with the vegetable oil and sesame oil. Season with salt and pepper to taste, and toss to coat. Spread in an even layer.

6 Place the meatballs on the lower rack and the broccoli on the upper rack of the oven. Bake for 10 minutes. Remove both pans. Using tongs, turn each meatball over. Stir the broccoli. Return the pans to the oven (in the same spots) and bake for 4 to 8 minutes longer, until the meatballs are cooked through and the broccoli is browned and tender.

7 Reheat the glaze, if needed. Transfer the meatballs to the glaze and stir to coat. Bring to a simmer and cook until the meatballs are coated and warmed through. Remove the pot from the heat and let sit for 5 minutes (the glaze will thicken slightly as it cools).

8 Transfer the broccoli to a bowl and drizzle with the remaining 1 teaspoon tamari. Sprinkle on the sesame seeds and toss to coat.

9 Spoon the grains into bowls. Arrange the meatballs (with the glaze) and broccoli over the top. Sprinkle with sliced scallions.

BOWLS

1 pound ground turkey (preferably dark meat)

⅓ cup panko breadcrumbs (regular or gluten-free)

1 scallion, thinly sliced, plus more for serving

1 large garlic clove, minced

2 teaspoons minced fresh gingerroot

3 teaspoons low-sodium tamari or soy sauce

1 egg, lightly beaten

Salt and freshly ground black pepper

1 large bunch broccoli, cut into florets (about 4 cups)

1 tablespoon neutral vegetable oil (such as grapeseed)

1 teaspoon toasted sesame oil

1 tablespoon toasted sesame seeds

1 batch cooked grains

CHICKEN BURRITO BOWLS
+ GUACAMOLE

We eat Mexican food for dinner at least once a week, a tradition that started when Ella was a toddler and tacos were one of the only ways we could get her to eat vegetables (as long as they were chopped up in a tortilla with cheese, she was happy). We always start with a big bowl of guacamole, which we snack on while cooking and then spoon over whatever we're making. These chicken burrito bowls are one of our very favorites.

Spice-rubbed chicken is paired with a warm bean and corn salad, along with shredded romaine lettuce and cheese. A scoop of guacamole and a drizzle of lime sour cream are the pièce de résistance. The recipe makes a big batch of guacamole, so feel free to halve it if you're not so avocado-obsessed. And in case you were wondering: yes, Ella still prefers hers wrapped in a tortilla.

For a vegetarian variation, swap out the chicken for firm tofu.

SERVES 4 | PREP TIME: 20 minutes | COOKING TIME: 15 minutes

MAKE THE GUACAMOLE

1 Scoop the avocado flesh into a bowl and add the garlic and lime juice. Mash everything together with a fork until creamy but still slightly chunky (or however you like it!). Season with salt and pepper, and fold in the cilantro to taste. Taste and add additional lime juice or seasonings, if desired.

MAKE THE LIME SOUR CREAM

2 Mix the sour cream with the lime zest and 2 teaspoons of the lime juice in a small bowl. Stir in the water, just until the sour cream is loose enough to drizzle (but is not watery). Season with salt and pepper to taste.

GUACAMOLE

- 2 ripe avocados, pitted
- 1 small garlic clove, grated on a Microplane
  Juice of ½ lime, plus more as needed
  Salt and freshly ground black pepper
- 1–2 tablespoons finely chopped fresh cilantro

LIME SOUR CREAM

- ½ cup sour cream
- ½ teaspoon lime zest
- 4 teaspoons lime juice
- 2–3 teaspoons water

MAKE-AHEAD OPTIONS

The guacamole can be refrigerated for up to 1 day. Place a piece of plastic wrap directly on the surface and cover it tightly to prevent browning (it may still brown slightly, but just scrape off any brown bits).

The lime sour cream can be refrigerated for up to 2 days.

Other Sauces to Try

- Fresh Tomato Salsa (page 55)
- Avocado, Corn & Tomato Relish (page 134)

RECIPE CONTINUES

BOWLS

- 1 tablespoon chili powder
- 1 teaspoon ground cumin
- ¾–1 pound boneless, skinless chicken thighs (or you can use boneless, skinless breasts, pounded ½ inch thick)

   Salt and freshly ground black pepper
- 2 tablespoons extra-virgin olive oil
- 1 small jalapeño, seeded and minced
- 1 garlic clove, minced
- 1 cup drained and rinsed black beans
- 1 cup fresh or frozen sweet corn
- 1 cup halved grape tomatoes
- 2 tablespoons coarsely chopped fresh cilantro, plus more for serving
- 1 batch cooked grains

TOPPINGS

   Shredded romaine lettuce

   Shredded cheddar or crumbled cotija cheese

   Hot sauce

   Corn tortilla chips

BUILD THE BOWLS

3 Stir together the chili powder and cumin in a small bowl. Season the chicken thighs on both sides with salt and pepper. Sprinkle them evenly with the spice mixture, patting to coat.

4 Heat the oil in a large nonstick or cast-iron skillet over medium-high heat. Add the chicken and cook, flipping once or twice and adjusting the heat as needed, until browned on both sides and cooked through, 6 to 7 minutes total (the internal temperature should read 165°F/74°C). Transfer the chicken to a cutting board.

5 Place the skillet back over medium heat and add the jalapeño and garlic. Cook, stirring, until fragrant. Add the beans and corn, and season with salt and pepper to taste. Cook, stirring, until warmed through, 1 to 2 minutes. Remove the pan from the heat and add the tomatoes. Stir in the remaining 2 teaspoons lime juice and the cilantro. Season with a bit more salt and pepper, and toss to coat.

6 Slice or chop the chicken.

7 Spoon the grains into bowls. Arrange the chicken over the top, along with the bean salad, a small pile of romaine, and a small pile of cheese. Spoon a generous (at least for me!) helping of the guacamole in each bowl and drizzle with the lime sour cream. Sprinkle with a bit of cilantro and then drizzle with hot sauce and arrange a few tortilla chips around the bowl.

CHILI POWDER

Chili powder is a blend of dried chiles and other spices, such as cumin, garlic, and oregano. Some brands are spicier than others, so give yours a taste before using. If it's quite spicy, feel free to cut back on the quantity. I use organic Frontier brand, which is mild but flavorful.

CHICKEN SAUSAGES
WITH BROCCOLI RABE & BURRATA + SUN-DRIED TOMATO PESTO

Let's be honest: you had me at burrata. Burrata is a fresh Italian mozzarella with cream in the center, and it's *to. die. for.* A few years ago, I ate an appetizer of garlicky broccoli rabe topped with a glistening ball of burrata at an Italian restaurant in New York City, and it quickly became a favorite combination. I think you'll love how the sweet creaminess of the cheese mellows out the slight bitterness of the greens (if you can't find burrata, fresh mozzarella is a great substitution).

Seared chicken sausages turn this into a full meal, and a sun-dried tomato pesto ties everything together. Don't be afraid of the anchovy in the broccoli rabe — it adds loads of depth, but you won't taste any fishiness.

For a vegetarian variation, swap out the chicken for sliced summer squash and/or zucchini and omit the anchovy.

SERVES 4 | PREP TIME: 15 minutes | COOKING TIME: 15 minutes

Salt

1 bunch broccoli rabe, tough bottom stems trimmed

3 tablespoons extra-virgin olive oil

2 garlic cloves, thinly sliced

1 or 2 anchovy fillets, rinsed and finely chopped

Freshly ground black pepper

2 teaspoons lemon juice

3 cooked chicken sausages, cut on the diagonal into ¼-inch-thick slices

1 batch cooked grains

Sun-Dried Tomato Pesto (page 102)

8 ounces fresh burrata (1 large ball)

1 Bring a large pot of water to a boil and season it generously with salt. Add the broccoli rabe and cook until it's bright green and tender (a knife should easily pass through the stems), about 2 minutes. Drain and rinse under cold water to stop the cooking. Pat dry.

2 Heat 2 tablespoons of the oil in a large skillet over medium heat. Add the garlic and anchovy (to taste). Cook, stirring, until the garlic is softened, 1 to 2 minutes. Add the broccoli rabe and season with salt and pepper to taste. Cook, tossing with tongs, until warmed through and tender, 2 to 3 minutes. Drizzle with the lemon juice. Transfer the broccoli rabe to a plate.

3 Using the same skillet, heat the remaining 1 tablespoon oil over medium-high heat. Add the sliced chicken sausages, spreading them in a single layer. Cook until lightly browned on both sides, 4 to 5 minutes total.

4 Spoon the grains into bowls. Add a spoonful or two of the pesto and toss to lightly coat the grains. Arrange the chicken sausage slices and broccoli rabe over the top. Carefully divide the burrata into four pieces (be mindful of that precious cream in the middle!) and arrange on top of the bowls. Serve with another spoonful of pesto.

Other Sauces to Try
- Classic Pesto (page 79)
- Salsa Verde (page 150)

Picky kids? Serve the components separately and let them build their own bowls.

CHICKEN, NAPA CABBAGE & SNOW PEAS + COCONUT-PEANUT SAUCE

This dinner is creamy, crunchy, sweet, salty, *and* spicy. In other words: it's heavenly. The sauce, made with peanut butter and coconut milk, is the real star of the show. It instantly dresses up chicken (you can use leftover cooked chicken here) and is a fantastic dressing for noodle salads and Asian slaws. It also makes a killer marinade — toss a pound of cubed chicken breasts or thighs with about ½ cup of the sauce (reserve the rest for serving) and refrigerate it for a few hours or overnight. Thread the chicken cubes onto skewers and grill them. For summer parties, pile the skewers on a platter, arrange the other components in dishes alongside, and then let your guests build their own bowls.

For a vegetarian variation, swap out the chicken for tofu.

SERVES 4 | PREP TIME: 30 minutes | COOKING TIME: 5 minutes

MAKE THE SAUCE

1 Place the coconut milk, lime juice, tamari, fish sauce, garlic, gingerroot, peanut butter, sugar, and 1 teaspoon of the sriracha in a blender. Season with salt and black pepper. Blend on high speed until smooth. Taste and season with additional sriracha, salt, black pepper, and/or lime juice, as needed.

BUILD THE BOWLS

2 Fill a saucepan with about 1 inch of water and bring to a simmer. Insert a steamer basket and add the snow peas. Cover and steam until bright green and tender crisp, about 2 minutes. Drain and rinse under cold water to stop the cooking. Pat dry.

3 Toss the cabbage and bell pepper with the lime juice and oil in a large bowl. Season with salt and black pepper to taste.

4 Spoon the grains into bowls. Arrange the snow peas, cabbage slaw, and chicken over the top. Drizzle with the coconut-peanut sauce and sprinkle with the cilantro, mint, and peanuts. Serve with sriracha, lime wedges, and additional sauce for drizzling.

MAKE-AHEAD OPTION

The sauce can be made up to 5 days in advance. Bring it to room temperature before serving. If needed, thin it with a drizzle of water.

COCONUT-PEANUT SAUCE

1 cup canned coconut milk (well stirred)

2 tablespoons lime juice

1 teaspoon low-sodium tamari or soy sauce

1 teaspoon fish sauce

2 garlic cloves, coarsely chopped

1 teaspoon coarsely chopped fresh gingerroot

½ cup peanut butter

1 tablespoon packed light brown sugar

1–2 teaspoons sriracha

Salt and freshly ground black pepper

BOWLS

1½ cups snow peas

1 heaping cup thinly sliced napa cabbage

½ red bell pepper, thinly sliced

Juice of ½ lime

1 teaspoon extra-virgin olive oil

Salt and freshly ground black pepper

1 batch cooked grains

2 cups chopped or cubed cooked chicken or tofu

TOPPINGS

Chopped fresh cilantro

Chopped fresh mint

Chopped roasted peanuts

Sriracha

Lime wedges

SAUSAGE MEATBALLS WITH FRESH RICOTTA
& CRISPY BROCCOLI + QUICK & EASY MARINARA SAUCE

SAUCE

- 1 (28-ounce) can whole peeled tomatoes (preferably San Marzano)
- 1 teaspoon extra-virgin olive oil
- 1 garlic clove, coarsely chopped
- ½ teaspoon sugar
- ⅛ teaspoon dried oregano

  Pinch of red pepper flakes

  Salt and freshly ground black pepper
- 1 tablespoon thinly sliced fresh basil

Meatballs with tomato sauce is one of my kids' top-five favorite meals, but it can be a hassle to make on weeknights as it often involves an arm's-length list of ingredients. Luckily for the girls (and me!), this hacked version, which simply uses fresh Italian chicken sausage and a five-minute marinara sauce, is easy enough for any Tuesday. All I do is shape the sausage (which is already perfectly seasoned) into meatballs and cook them in the sauce.

My family is *hooked*. We serve the meatballs with crispy broccoli, which my girls love to dip in the marinara, and a dollop of fresh ricotta cheese (see box, below). Chewy grains, such as sorghum, any of the wheat berries, or barley, are particularly delicious here (as is pasta or polenta).

SERVES 4 | PREP TIME: 15 minutes | COOKING TIME: 30 minutes

MAKE THE SAUCE

1 Drain the tomatoes over a bowl (you're just aiming to drain off the watery liquid — it's okay if there's still some thick purée around the tomatoes). Place the drained tomatoes and 2 tablespoons of the liquid from the bowl in a blender along with the oil, garlic, sugar, oregano, and pepper flakes. Season with salt and black pepper to taste. Blend on high speed until smooth. Add the basil and pulse to combine.

FRESH RICOTTA

Not all ricotta cheese is created equal. For this recipe (and, I'd argue, for any recipe), you want to seek out high-quality brands that list only milk (and/or whey), salt, and vinegar in the ingredient list — no stabilizers or gums. It should taste sweet and creamy. You can find the ultra-good stuff (which you will want to eat with a spoon) at Italian markets and specialty cheese stores, but some solid supermarket brands include Organic Valley, Calabro, and Biazzo.

BUILD THE BOWLS

2 Preheat the oven to 425°F (220°C). Line a baking sheet with aluminum foil.

3 Place the broccoli on the baking sheet and toss with 2 tablespoons of the oil. Season with salt and black pepper. Roast for 15 to 20 minutes, until browned and crispy around the edges, stirring once.

4 In the meantime, shape the sausages into 1½-inch meatballs. Heat the remaining 1 tablespoon oil in a large skillet over medium-high heat. Working in batches, brown the meatballs on all sides, 6 to 8 minutes total. Spoon off and discard any fat in the skillet. Carefully pour in the tomato sauce (stand back, it might sputter!). Bring the sauce to a simmer and cook, stirring occasionally, until the sauce is slightly thickened and the meatballs are cooked through, 10 to 15 minutes.

5 Spoon the grains into bowls. Arrange the meatballs and sauce over the grains, along with the crispy broccoli. Sprinkle with grated Parmesan and add a big dollop of ricotta. Sprinkle with basil.

BOWLS

1 large bunch broccoli, cut into small florets (about 4 cups)

3 tablespoons extra-virgin olive oil

Salt and freshly ground black pepper

12 ounces fresh Italian chicken sausages, casings removed

1 batch cooked grains

Grated Parmesan cheese, for serving

Fresh ricotta cheese, for serving

Sliced fresh basil, for serving

MAKE-AHEAD OPTION

The sauce can be refrigerated for up to 1 week or frozen for up to 3 months.

CRUNCHY VIETNAMESE-INSPIRED CHICKEN & RICE SALAD + SPICY LIME DRESSING

Flavor bomb. That should be the name of this salad. When I was in my early 20s, my husband and I lived in New York City in a tiny railroad-style apartment, and we'd regularly order Vietnamese food, which is one of my favorite cuisines — it's utterly fresh, with loads of herbs and contrasting textures. I often incorporate some of the cuisine's flavors into our dinners.

This salad is one of our favorites, featuring a serrano-spiked dressing, cooked shredded chicken (this is a great way to use up leftovers), cabbage, and carrots, along with loads of mint, cilantro, and peanuts. The bowls are topped with fried shallots, which are nutty, crispy, and totally addicting, although you can omit them if you're pressed for time. I love this salad with black rice for the contrast in color, but any rice will do.

For a vegetarian variation, swap out the chicken for sautéed tofu.

SERVES 4–6 | PREP TIME: 35 minutes | COOKING TIME: 5 minutes

MAKE THE DRESSING

1 Combine the garlic, oil, vinegar, lime juice, honey, and fish sauce in a mini food processor or small blender. Blend until smooth. Stir in the chiles.

BUILD THE BOWLS

2 If you're frying the shallots (good for you!), heat ¼ inch of oil in a medium skillet over medium heat until shimmering. Set a strainer over a bowl (this will be to drain the shallots later). Add a single shallot ring to the hot oil — if it starts bubbling immediately, you're good to add the rest (if not, let the oil continue to heat). Cook, stirring constantly, until the shallots are golden brown, 4 to 5 minutes. Drain the shallots in the strainer over the bowl and then transfer them to paper towels to drain further. Season with salt to taste.

3 Combine the rice, cabbage, carrots, chicken, cilantro, mint, and peanuts in a large bowl. Add the dressing and toss to combine. Season with salt and pepper to taste. Top with the fried shallots, if using, and serve with lime wedges.

SPICY LIME DRESSING

- 4 garlic cloves, coarsely chopped
- ¼ cup plus 2 tablespoons neutral vegetable oil (such as grapeseed)
- 3 tablespoons rice vinegar
- 3 tablespoons lime juice
- 3 tablespoons honey
- 2–3 tablespoons fish sauce, as desired (I use 3 tablespoons of Red Boat brand, which is milder than others)
- 1 or 2 serrano chiles, thinly sliced, as desired (depending on how spicy you like it)

BOWLS

- Neutral vegetable oil (such as grapeseed), for frying (optional)
- 2 large shallots, very thinly sliced (optional)
- Salt
- 1 batch cooked rice, preferably black (cooled)
- ¼ medium green cabbage, very finely sliced (about 4 cups)
- 2 large carrots, shredded (about 1 cup)
- 3 cups cooked, shredded chicken
- ½ cup coarsely chopped fresh cilantro
- ½ cup coarsely chopped fresh mint
- ½ cup coarsely chopped roasted peanuts
- Freshly ground black pepper
- Lime wedges, for serving

THAI-INSPIRED TURKEY FRIED RICE

SAUCE

1½–2½ tablespoons fish sauce (I use 2½ tablespoons of Red Boat brand, which is milder than others), plus more for serving

1 tablespoon rice vinegar

1 tablespoon honey

⅛ teaspoon red pepper flakes

BOWLS

3 tablespoons neutral vegetable oil (such as grapeseed)

6 scallions, thinly sliced, plus more for serving

3 medium carrots, shredded on a box grater or in a food processor

4 garlic cloves, minced

1 pound ground turkey

Salt and freshly ground black pepper

1 batch cooked rice (cooled)

½ cup frozen peas or cooked fresh peas

TOPPINGS

Coarsely chopped roasted peanuts

Sliced jalapeño

Lime wedges

Tomato wedges (optional)

This isn't your typical Chinese-style fried rice, but I have to admit, I like it even better. This version takes inspiration from Thai fried rice, which is flavored with garlic, fish sauce, and rice vinegar. It's light but satisfying, with a salty-sweet edge. The fried rice is topped with roasted peanuts and spicy jalapeño slices (or you could use red pepper flakes or sriracha) for heat. Juicy tomato slices, which are commonly served with Thai fried rice, offer a sweet counterpoint, but they're optional.

Be sure to prep your ingredients before beginning, as the cooking process goes rather quickly. Also, the rice (I prefer brown rice) should be completely cooled or even cold, otherwise it will get mushy. To cool it quickly, spread the cooked rice on a baking sheet and refrigerate until cold (or use day-old rice).

For a vegetarian option, swap out the turkey for tofu or meat-free crumbles.

SERVES 4 | PREP TIME: 15 minutes | COOKING TIME: 10 minutes

1 Mix 1½ tablespoons of the fish sauce with the vinegar, honey, and pepper flakes in a small bowl. Set aside.

2 Heat 2 tablespoons of the oil in a 12-inch skillet or large wok over medium-high heat. Add the scallions, carrots, and garlic, and cook, stirring, until fragrant and lightly softened, about 2 minutes. Push the vegetables to one side of the skillet or wok and add the turkey to the other side. Season with salt and black pepper. Cook, breaking up the meat with a wooden spoon, until it starts to brown. Incorporate it with the vegetables and cook, stirring everything, until the meat is cooked through.

3 Add the remaining 1 tablespoon oil, followed by the rice and peas. Cook, stirring, until the rice and peas are heated through, about 2 minutes. Pour in the fish sauce mixture and toss to coat. Remove the pan from the heat and give the fried rice a taste. Drizzle in the remaining 1 tablespoon fish sauce, if desired (different brands vary in their intensity), and season with salt and pepper, if needed.

4 Spoon the fried rice into bowls and sprinkle with sliced scallions, peanuts, and a few slices of jalapeño. Serve with lime wedges and tomato wedges (if using), along with extra fish sauce, for those who like it punchy.

ZA'ATAR CHICKEN WITH ROASTED CAULIFLOWER & POMEGRANATE MOLASSES

Za'atar is a Moroccan spice blend of sumac, cumin, sesame seeds, and other spices. It's traditionally baked into breads, served with olive oil as a dipping sauce, or used as a seasoning. I love its smoky, tart flavor and sprinkle it on everything from vegetables to hummus to meat. It adds loads of flavor to this quick marinade for chicken thighs, which are served alongside caramelized cauliflower and labneh or Greek yogurt. The bowls are garnished with a drizzle of sweet-tart pomegranate molasses, toasted pine nuts, pomegranate seeds, and fresh mint or cilantro. It's utterly simple but irresistibly complex.

SERVES 4 | PREP TIME: 10 minutes | COOKING TIME: 40 minutes

1 Preheat the oven to 425°F (220°C).

2 Place the cauliflower florets on a large baking sheet and toss with 2 tablespoons of the oil. Season with salt and pepper. Roast, stirring once or twice, for 30 to 35 minutes, until the cauliflower is caramelized and tender.

3 In the meantime, combine the garlic, gingerroot, za'atar, lemon juice, and the remaining 2 tablespoons oil in a large bowl. Add the chicken and season with salt and pepper. Toss to coat evenly. Let sit at room temperature for 15 to 30 minutes.

4 Preheat a grill or grill pan to medium-high heat, and brush with oil (alternatively, you can cook the chicken in batches in a large skillet).

5 Cook the chicken on both sides until browned and cooked through (the internal temperature should read 165°F/74°C), 3 to 5 minutes per side, depending on the thickness of the chicken. Transfer to a cutting board and let rest for 5 minutes. Slice the chicken against the grain.

6 Spoon the grains into bowls. Arrange the chicken and cauliflower in each bowl, along with a spoonful of labneh. Drizzle everything with pomegranate molasses and sprinkle with za'atar. Top with pine nuts, pomegranate seeds, and mint.

1 head cauliflower, cut into 1-inch florets

4 tablespoons extra-virgin olive oil

Salt and freshly ground black pepper

2 garlic cloves, grated

1 tablespoon grated fresh gingerroot

1 tablespoon za'atar, plus more for serving

2 tablespoons lemon juice

1¼ pounds boneless, skinless chicken thighs

1 batch cooked grains

TOPPINGS

Labneh or Greek yogurt

Pomegranate molasses

Toasted pine nuts

Pomegranate seeds

Coarsely chopped fresh mint and/or cilantro

POMEGRANATE MOLASSES

Pomegranate molasses is made by boiling down pomegranate juice into a thick red syrup. It's both sweet and tart, and it's delicious drizzled over chicken, lamb, rice, pancakes, or yogurt. You can also add it to sauces or salad dressings for a sweet-and-sour kick. Find it at specialty grocery stores or online.

DECONSTRUCTED (AND LIGHTENED-UP)
PORK BANH MI BOWLS + SRIRACHA-MAPLE YOGURT

MARINADE

- 3 tablespoons maple syrup
- 2–3 tablespoons Asian fish sauce
- 2 tablespoons low-sodium tamari or soy sauce
- 1 tablespoon neutral vegetable oil (such as grapeseed)
- 1 teaspoon sriracha
- 3 scallions, coarsely chopped
- 2 garlic cloves, coarsely chopped
- 1 teaspoon grated fresh gingerroot
- 1–1¼ pounds pork tenderloin

PICKLED VEGGIES

- 4 medium red radishes, halved and very thinly sliced
- 1 medium carrot, shredded
- ½ small English cucumber, halved and very thinly sliced
- 3 tablespoons rice vinegar
- 2 teaspoons sugar
- ¾ teaspoon kosher salt
- Pinch of gochugaru (page 52) or red pepper flakes, or as desired

BOWLS

- 1 batch cooked rice
- 1 jalapeño, thinly sliced
- ½ cup lightly packed fresh cilantro leaves
- Maple-Sriracha Yogurt (page 67)

A Vietnamese banh mi sandwich is a thing of beauty. It can be made in myriad ways, but typically it's a French baguette stuffed with roasted pork, pâté, pickled vegetables, cilantro, and a chile-spiked mayonnaise. This meal uses similar flavors but with a lighter — although no less satisfying — result. Thinly sliced pork tenderloin quickly soaks up an umami-packed marinade of fish sauce, tamari, maple syrup, garlic, and gingerroot before being caramelized in a hot pan. The salty pork is counterbalanced by a slightly sweet pickled salad, fresh cilantro, and slices of jalapeño.

Instead of the traditional mayo sauce, I drizzle the bowls with a lighter sriracha-maple yogurt, lending creaminess and heat. We crave this meal, and I think you will, too. Rice is my grain of choice with these bowls.

SERVES 4 | PREP TIME: 40 minutes | COOKING TIME: 10 minutes

1 Purée the maple syrup, fish sauce (I use 3 tablespoons of Red Boat brand, which is milder than others), tamari, oil, sriracha, scallions, garlic, and gingerroot in a blender.

2 Slice the pork tenderloin crosswise (against the grain) on the diagonal into ½-inch pieces. Flatten each piece using the palm of your hand (you can place the meat between layers of plastic wrap or use disposable kitchen gloves if you don't want to get your hands dirty). Transfer the meat to a bowl. Pour the marinade from the blender over the pork, tossing well to coat. Let sit at room temperature for 15 to 30 minutes.

3 Place the radishes, carrot, and cucumber in a heatproof bowl. Bring the vinegar, sugar, salt, and gochugaru to a boil in a small saucepan, stirring to dissolve the sugar. Pour the mixture over the vegetables and toss to coat. Let sit, stirring occasionally, while you cook the pork.

4 Lightly oil a large grill pan or cast-iron skillet and place it over medium-high heat (I prefer to use a pan instead of an outdoor grill, as the marinade tends to flare up on the grill). Working in batches, pull the pieces of pork out of the marinade, letting any excess liquid drip back into the bowl, and arrange them in a single layer in the pan. Cook until lightly browned on both sides and cooked through, 1 to 2 minutes per side. Transfer to a plate.

5 Spoon the rice into bowls. Arrange the meat and pickled vegetables over each bowl, and top with jalapeño slices and cilantro leaves. Drizzle with the maple-sriracha yogurt.

Other Sauces to Try
- Gochujang Sauce (page 137)

PORK TENDERLOIN WITH WARM RED CABBAGE
& APPLE SALAD + APPLE CIDER PAN SAUCE

PORK TENDERLOIN

1–1¼ pounds pork tenderloin, trimmed

Salt and freshly ground black pepper

2 teaspoons minced fresh rosemary

2 teaspoons minced fresh thyme

1 tablespoon extra-virgin olive oil

SALAD

3 tablespoons extra-virgin olive oil

1 large garlic clove, thinly sliced

½ small red onion, thinly sliced

Salt and freshly ground black pepper

¼ medium red cabbage, cored and thinly sliced (4 cups)

2 tablespoons apple cider vinegar, plus more as needed

½ green apple, finely diced

⅓ cup toasted walnuts, coarsely chopped

1 tablespoon chopped fresh flat-leaf parsley, plus more for serving

½ cup crumbled feta cheese

1 teaspoon cornstarch

1 cup plus 1 tablespoon apple cider

3 tablespoons crème fraîche

1 batch cooked grains

My favorite chunky gray sweater. Crackling leaves. Cider doughnuts. Pork tenderloin with apple cider pan sauce. These are my must-haves once the weather turns chilly. Here a pork tenderloin is rolled in fresh rosemary and thyme and then browned, roasted, and finished with a quick pan sauce made with apple cider and crème fraîche.

The pork is paired with a delicious feta-studded warm cabbage and apple salad, which I adapted from Deborah Madison's cookbook *Vegetarian Cooking for Everyone*. You'll want to pull on your cozy socks, pour a glass of wine, and listen to the leaves rustling outside the windows for this meal.

SERVES 4 | PREP TIME: 25 minutes | COOKING TIME: 30 minutes

1 Preheat the oven to 425°F (220°C).

2 Pat the pork tenderloin dry with paper towels and season it all over with salt and pepper. Sprinkle with the rosemary and thyme, pressing to adhere. Let sit for 10 to 15 minutes.

3 Heat the oil in a large ovenproof skillet over medium-high heat. Add the pork and cook, turning occasionally, until browned on all sides, 8 to 10 minutes total. Transfer the skillet to the oven and cook for 15 to 20 minutes, until an instant-read thermometer inserted into the thickest part of the pork reads 145°F (63°C).

4 While the pork cooks, make the salad. Heat the oil in a large skillet over medium heat. Add the garlic and onion, and season with salt and pepper. Cook, stirring occasionally, until the onion is softened but not browned, about 3 minutes. Add the cabbage and season with more salt and pepper. Cook, stirring occasionally, until the cabbage begins to soften and lighten in color, about 2 minutes. Stir in the vinegar and cook for a few more seconds. Remove the pan from the heat and add the apple, walnuts, and parsley. Season with salt and pepper, and toss to coat. Taste and season with more vinegar, salt, or pepper, if needed. Transfer to a bowl and let cool slightly. Sprinkle with the crumbled feta.

5 Combine the cornstarch with 1 tablespoon of the apple cider in a small bowl. Stir to dissolve.

6 Once the pork is cooked, transfer it to a cutting board. Carefully pour the remaining 1 cup apple cider into the skillet and place it over medium-high heat. Bring the cider to a boil, using a wooden spoon to scrape up any brown bits on the bottom of the pan. Cook until the cider is reduced by half, about 5 minutes. Whisk in the crème fraîche and bring the sauce to a simmer. Whisk in the cornstarch mixture. Bring to a simmer and cook until thickened (it should coat the back of a spoon). Season with salt and pepper to taste.

7 Slice the pork crosswise.

8 Spoon the grains into bowls. Arrange the pork in the bowls and drizzle with the pan sauce. Sprinkle with a bit of parsley. Pile the cabbage salad alongside. Serve with any remaining pan sauce.

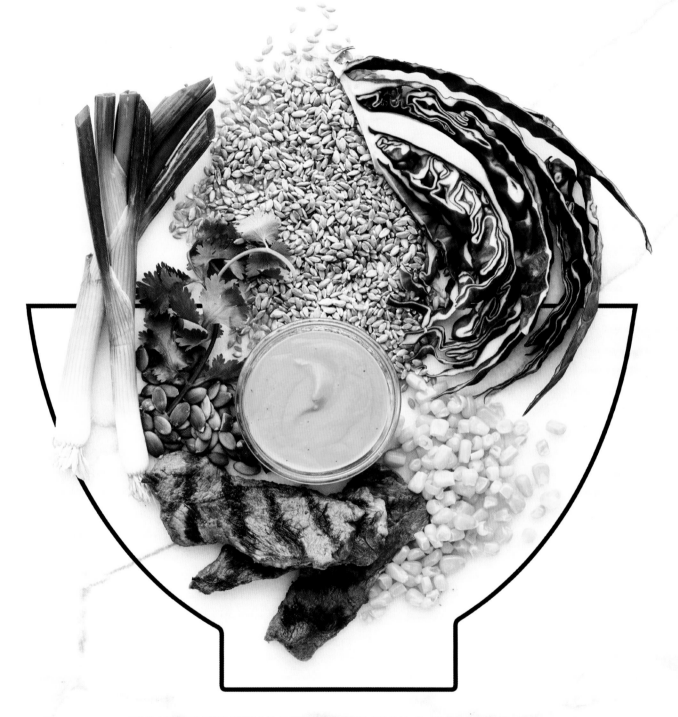

GRILLED SKIRT STEAK WITH SWEET CORN & CABBAGE SLAW +
ROASTED RED PEPPER & CASHEW SAUCE, PAGE 141

⑧
BEEF & LAMB

Ask me about some of the best meals I've had in my life, and I will tell you about the flavors on the following pages. Cinnamon- and allspice-scented lamb kofte with a cool yogurt sauce, Korean bibimbap-style steak bowls with kimchi, Italian-style pan-roasted steak with a garlicky salsa verde, chipotle-marinated hanger steak with an avocado, corn, and tomato relish . . . these are the dishes that transport me to some of my best food memories, from New York City to Tuscany to my mom's kitchen in Illinois.

But you don't need a plane ticket or even a lot of time to get there. In less than an hour, you can create meals that will not only get you out of your weeknight cooking rut but that might also jet you off to a new destination. Who knows, maybe you'll create some memories of your own along the way.

ASIAN LETTUCE WRAPS

This is one of our weeknight staples and one of Ella's most requested dinners. Naturally lean ground bison (or lean ground beef) is sautéed with onion, bell pepper, gingerroot, and garlic, then simmered in a quick, Asian-inspired sauce of tamari, fish sauce, sesame oil, brown sugar, and chicken broth. The meat is completely irresistible, and you might find yourself sneaking spoonfuls straight from the skillet like Juniper is apt to do (don't worry, I won't tell).

It is served over rice, with sriracha, cilantro, and peanuts, and then everything is tucked into lettuce leaves and rolled up like tacos. It's a messy, soul-satisfying type of meal that might just become a staple in your house, too.

SERVES 4 | **PREP TIME:** 15 minutes | **COOKING TIME:** 15–20 minutes

MAKE THE SAUCE

1 Whisk together the chicken broth, tamari, fish sauce (I use 2 teaspoons of Red Boat brand, which is milder than others), sugar, sesame oil, and cornstarch.

MAKE THE MEAT

2 Heat the olive oil in a large skillet over medium-high heat. Add the onion and bell pepper and cook, stirring, until softened, 3 to 5 minutes. Stir in the garlic, gingerroot, and tomato paste. Cook, stirring, for 1 minute.

3 Add the bison and season with salt and black pepper. Cook, breaking up the meat with a wooden spoon, until browned, about 3 minutes. Stir in the chicken broth mixture, and use a wooden spoon to scrape up any brown bits from the bottom of the skillet. Bring to a boil, then reduce the heat to a simmer. Cook until slightly thickened, 3 to 5 minutes. Add a dash or two (or three or four . . .) of sriracha. Remove the pot from the heat and add the lime zest, lime juice, and cilantro. Taste and season with additional sriracha and/or lime juice, if desired.

4 Spoon the grains into bowls. Top with the meat mixture. Sprinkle with cilantro and peanuts, and drizzle with sriracha, if you'd like. Serve with lettuce leaves for wrapping.

MAKE-AHEAD OPTION

The beef mixture can be refrigerated for up to 3 days. Reheat gently in a skillet.

SAUCE

- ½ cup low-sodium chicken broth
- 2 tablespoons low-sodium tamari or soy sauce
- 1–2 teaspoons fish sauce, as desired
- 2 teaspoons packed brown sugar or honey
- 1 teaspoon toasted sesame oil
- 2 teaspoons cornstarch

MEAT

- 1 tablespoon extra-virgin olive oil
- ½ medium onion, finely chopped
- ½ medium red bell pepper, seeded and finely diced
- 2 large garlic cloves, minced
- 1 tablespoon minced fresh gingerroot
- 1 tablespoon tomato paste
- 1 pound ground bison or lean ground beef

  Salt and freshly ground black pepper

  Sriracha or hot sauce
- ½ teaspoon lime zest

  Juice of ½ lime
- ¼ cup coarsely chopped fresh cilantro

TOPPINGS

- 1 batch cooked rice or quinoa

  Chopped cilantro

  Chopped peanuts or cashews
- 1 head Bibb or Boston lettuce, leaves separated

CHIPOTLE-MARINATED HANGER STEAK
WITH AVOCADO, CORN & TOMATO RELISH

AVOCADO, CORN & TOMATO RELISH

- 2 tablespoons lime juice
- 1 garlic clove, grated on a Microplane
- 2 cups raw or cooked corn kernels (from about 2 ears)
- 1 cup halved grape tomatoes
- ½ jalapeño, seeded and minced
- 2 scallions, thinly sliced
- ¼ cup coarsely chopped fresh cilantro
- 1 tablespoon extra-virgin olive oil
- 1 avocado, pitted, peeled, and diced

  Salt and freshly ground black pepper

Other Sauces to Try
- Guacamole (page 115)
- Fresh Tomato Salsa (page 55)

This is one of our favorite party meals, as it can be easily scaled up to feed a crowd. Hanger steak (or you can use skirt steak or even chicken thighs) is marinated in a mix of chipotle chiles, loads of garlic, orange juice, and brown sugar, creating a slightly spicy and sweet crust once grilled. It's served with a quick avocado, sweet corn, and tomato relish, which is amazing in its own right as a side dish or as an appetizer with tortilla chips.

You can use either raw sweet corn straight off the cob or cooked corn (in a pinch, you can even use thawed frozen supersweet corn). You'll want to start the steak marinating first, and then make the relish. A few slivers of vinegary radishes over the tops of the bowls make everything pop.

SERVES 4 | PREP TIME: 45 minutes | COOKING TIME: 15 minutes

MAKE THE RELISH

1 Combine the lime juice and garlic in a large bowl and let sit for 5 minutes (this will mellow out the garlic). Stir in the corn, tomatoes, jalapeño, scallions, cilantro, and olive oil. Fold in the avocado and season with salt and pepper. Taste and adjust the seasonings as needed.

HANGER STEAK

Also referred to as butcher's steak or bistro steak, hanger steak has a deep, meaty flavor and a tender texture. However, it's important to trim it properly. The whole steak comes as two muscles connected by a line of connective tissue down the center, with silver skin all around it. If you buy it from a good butcher, the silver skin and connective tissue will most likely be trimmed off, but if not, you'll want to do it at home, otherwise your steak will be tough.

To remove the silver skin, slide a thin, sharp knife under the silver skin, then grab it by the edge. Holding the silver skin taut with one hand, swipe your knife underneath it with the other hand to separate it from the meat. To remove the connective tissue, cut the steak in half lengthwise along the sinew to make two steaks, then trim away any white sinew from each.

BUILD THE BOWLS

2 Process the garlic cloves in a mini food processor until finely chopped. Add the chipotle chiles and adobo sauce, sugar, 2 tablespoons of the vegetable oil, and the orange juice, and season with salt and pepper. Process until mostly smooth. Place the steak in a large ziplock plastic bag and scrape in the marinade. Seal the bag and massage the contents to evenly coat the meat. Let sit at room temperature for 30 minutes (or up to 1 hour), turning the bag occasionally.

3 Preheat a grill or grill pan to medium-high heat.

4 Place the radishes in a small bowl and pour the vinegar over. Let sit, stirring occasionally.

5 Drizzle the onion rings with the remaining 1 tablespoon vegetable oil, rubbing it on both sides to lightly coat. Season with salt and pepper. Grill the onions until lightly charred on both sides, 3 to 4 minutes per side.

6 Remove the steak from the marinade, letting the marinade drip off. Grill the steak until browned with grill marks on the bottom, 3 to 5 minutes. Flip and cook until browned on the other side, 3 to 5 minutes longer for medium-rare. Transfer to a cutting board and let rest for 5 to 10 minutes. Thinly slice the meat against the grain.

7 Spoon the grains into bowls. Arrange the steak and onions in each bowl and top with the relish. Drain the radishes and top each bowl with a few radish slices.

BOWLS

4 garlic cloves, peeled

2 chipotle chiles in adobo, plus 1 tablespoon of adobo sauce from the can

1 tablespoon packed brown sugar

3 tablespoons neutral vegetable oil (such as grapeseed)

2 tablespoons orange juice

Salt and freshly ground black pepper

1 pound hanger steak, trimmed (see tip, opposite), or 1 pound skirt steak, cut crosswise into 2 or 3 pieces

2 medium radishes, very thinly sliced

¼ cup rice vinegar

1 large sweet onion, cut into ¼-inch-thick rings (keep the rings intact)

1 batch cooked grains

135

> ### MAKE-AHEAD OPTION
>
> For even more flavor, marinate the steak overnight in the refrigerator.

BIBIMBAP-STYLE STEAK
WITH BOK CHOY, CARROTS & KIMCHI + GOCHUJANG SAUCE

These Korean-inspired bowls are perfect both in the height of summer, when we practically live out by our grill, and in the doldrums of winter, when we crave foods that are spicy and revitalizing. Thinly sliced flank steak soaks up a robust marinade of tamari, garlic, sesame oil, and brown sugar and takes only minutes to grill. The steak is layered in bowls with sesame carrots, garlicky bok choy (both of which can be cooked in a cast-iron skillet right on the grill, if you're cooking outside), kimchi, and a spicy-sweet gochujang sauce.

If you want to take the bowls over the top, slide on a fried egg before serving.

For a vegetarian variation, swap out the beef for tofu or sliced portobello mushrooms.

SERVES 4 | **PREP TIME:** 25 minutes | **COOKING TIME:** 20 minutes

MAKE THE SAUCE

1 Combine the gochujang, tamari, vinegar, oil, and sugar in a small bowl.

MAKE THE MARINADE

2 Combine the tamari, oil, gochugaru, and sugar in a medium bowl. Add the grated garlic and whisk until the sugar is dissolved. Add the sliced flank steak and toss to coat. Let sit at room temperature for 15 to 30 minutes.

SLICING THE STEAK

To make it easier to thinly slice the flank steak, pop it in the freezer for 10 to 15 minutes to firm up. Use your longest, thinnest knife, and be sure to slice against the grain of the meat (in other words, slice cross-wise), which will give you more tender results.

SPICE SUB

Gochujang is a Korean chili paste that lends loads of earthy, umami flavor to the sauce, but if you can't find it you can omit the sauce altogether and drizzle the bowls with sriracha instead.

GOCHUJANG SAUCE

- ¼ cup gochujang
- 2 tablespoons low-sodium tamari or soy sauce
- 1 tablespoon rice vinegar
- 1 teaspoon toasted sesame oil
- 2 tablespoons packed light brown sugar

MARINADE

- ¼ cup low-sodium tamari or soy sauce
- 1 tablespoon toasted sesame oil
- 1 teaspoon gochugaru or ½ teaspoon red pepper flakes
- 1 teaspoon packed light brown sugar
- 4 large garlic cloves, 2 grated on a Microplane and 2 thinly sliced
- 1 pound flank steak, cut against the grain into ¼-inch-thick slices

MAKE-AHEAD OPTIONS

The gochujang sauce can be up to 5 days in advance.

The marinated steak can be refrigerated for up to 1 day.

RECIPE CONTINUES

BOWLS

2 tablespoons toasted sesame oil

4 heads baby bok choy, thinly sliced

Salt and freshly ground black pepper

1 lime, halved

3 medium carrots, thinly sliced on the diagonal

1 teaspoon toasted sesame seeds

4 eggs (optional)

1 batch cooked rice or quinoa

Kimchi, for serving

4 eggs (optional)

2 scallions, thinly sliced

BUILD THE BOWLS

3 Heat 1 tablespoon of the oil in a large nonstick skillet over medium heat. Add the sliced garlic and cook, stirring, until fragrant, about 45 seconds. Pile in the bok choy and season with salt and pepper. Cook, stirring occasionally, until tender crisp, about 3 minutes. Squeeze in the juice from ½ lime and season with salt and pepper to taste. Transfer the bok choy to a plate or bowl.

4 Heat the remaining 1 tablespoon oil in the same skillet over medium heat. Add the carrots and season with salt and pepper. Cook, stirring occasionally, until tender, 3 to 5 minutes. Squeeze in the juice from the remaining ½ lime. Scrape the carrots into a bowl and add the sesame seeds. Toss to combine.

5 Preheat a grill or grill pan over high heat and brush it with oil (alternatively, you can cook the steak on a large griddle over high heat).

6 Season the steak lightly with salt and pepper, and toss to coat. Working in batches, lay the steak slices flat on the grill in a single layer. Cook until browned on the bottom, 30 to 60 seconds. Flip and cook until browned on the other side but still pink in spots in the middle, 30 to 60 seconds longer. Transfer to a plate. Continue with the remaining steak (if using an outdoor grill, close the lid between batches to bring the heat back up).

7 Fry the eggs, if using.

8 Spoon the grains into bowls. Arrange the steak, bok choy, and carrots over the top, along with a spoonful of kimchi. Drizzle the bowls with the gochujang sauce. Top each bowl with a fried egg, if desired. Sprinkle with the scallions. Serve with additional sauce and kimchi at the table.

LIGHTENED-UP CHILI BOWLS

I grew up in the Midwest, where chili is a staple once football season begins. Although I was the bookworm reading on the couch while my brothers and Dad hollered at the Bears, I was a big fan of my mom's piping-hot bowls of meat and beans, usually served straight from the slow cooker.

My healthier version goes lighter on the meat and heavier on the vegetables but has a rich, robust flavor thanks to two secret ingredients: cacao powder and cinnamon. You won't taste them in the chili, but they add warmth and complexity, giving it a cooked-all-day flavor even though it comes together in less than an hour. Be sure to chop the vegetables nice and small so that they cook quickly and evenly. The chili tastes even better the next day.

SERVES 4–6 | PREP TIME: 20 minutes | COOKING TIME: 25 minutes

1 Combine the chili powder, cacao powder, cumin, oregano, and cinnamon in a small bowl. Set aside.

2 Heat 1 tablespoon of the oil in a large, straight-sided skillet (or you can use a large pot) over medium-high heat. Add the beef and season with salt and black pepper. Cook, stirring occasionally, until browned, 3 to 4 minutes. Transfer to a plate.

3 Place the skillet back over medium-high heat and swirl in the remaining 1 tablespoon oil. Add the onion, bell pepper, and carrot, and season with salt and black pepper. Cook, stirring occasionally, until the vegetables are tender, 4 to 5 minutes. Stir in the jalapeño and garlic, followed by the tomato paste and the reserved spice mixture. Cook, stirring, for 30 seconds.

4 Scrape the meat back into the skillet and add the tomatoes with their liquid, chicken broth, and beans. Season with salt and black pepper. Bring to a boil, then reduce the heat to a simmer and cook, stirring occasionally, until the vegetables are tender and the chili has thickened slightly, 10 to 15 minutes. Season with salt and black pepper, and squeeze in the juice from ½ lime.

5 Spoon the grains into bowls, and ladle the chili over the top. Serve with the toppings of your choice, such as shredded cheese, Greek yogurt, avocado, sliced scallions, and hot sauce. Serve with lime wedges.

SPICE MIXTURE

- 1 tablespoon chili powder
- 1 tablespoon raw cacao powder or unsweetened cocoa powder
- 1 teaspoon ground cumin
- ½ teaspoon dried oregano
- ¼ teaspoon ground cinnamon

CHILI

- 2 tablespoons extra-virgin olive oil
- 12 ounces lean ground beef
  Salt and freshly ground black pepper
- 1 small onion, finely chopped
- 1 small red bell pepper, finely chopped
- 1 small carrot, finely chopped
- 1 jalapeño, seeded and minced
- 2 garlic cloves, minced
- 1 tablespoon tomato paste
- 1 (15-ounce) can diced tomatoes
- 2 cups low-sodium chicken broth
- 1 (15-ounce) can pinto beans, rinsed and drained
  Juice of ½ lime
- 1 batch cooked quinoa, rice, or millet

TOPPINGS

Shredded cheddar cheese

Greek yogurt or sour cream

Diced avocado

Sliced scallions

Hot sauce

Lime wedges

GRILLED SKIRT STEAK WITH SWEET CORN & CABBAGE SLAW + ROASTED RED PEPPER & CASHEW SAUCE

These bowls are a deconstructed version of our favorite skirt steak tostadas recipe, which comes from *Bon Appétit* magazine. Luckily for me, the bowl version is easier, healthier, and (dare I say!) tastier than its tostada sibling. Skirt steak is rubbed with spices and then grilled and served with a jaunty red cabbage and sweet corn slaw.

You could stop there and have a really fine meal, but I like to take things over the top and drizzle the bowls with a satiny red pepper–cashew sauce, which brightens up the bowls and ties the whole meal together.

For a vegetarian variation, use firm tofu in place of the skirt steak.

SERVES 4 | PREP TIME: 20 minutes, plus 4–12 hours to soak the cashews
COOKING TIME: 30 minutes

MAKE THE STEAK

1 Season the pieces of steak on both sides with salt and pepper, and sprinkle with the cumin and granulated garlic.

2 Preheat a grill or grill pan to medium-high heat.

3 Brush the grill with oil. Grill the steak until browned with grill marks on the bottom, 3 to 4 minutes. Flip and cook until browned on the other side, 3 to 4 minutes longer for medium-rare. Transfer to a cutting board and let rest for 5 to 10 minutes.

MAKE THE SLAW

4 Whisk together the mayonnaise and lime juice in a large bowl. Season with salt and pepper. Add the cabbage, corn, scallion, and cilantro. Season with a bit more salt and pepper, and toss to coat.

BUILD THE BOWLS

5 Spoon the grains into bowls. Thinly slice the steak against the grain. Arrange the steak and cabbage slaw over each bowl. Drizzle with the sauce, and sprinkle with pepitas.

STEAK

- 1 skirt steak (1–1½ pounds), cut crosswise into 3 or 4 pieces
- Salt and freshly ground black pepper
- 1 teaspoon ground cumin
- 1 teaspoon granulated garlic or garlic powder

SLAW

- 2 tablespoons mayonnaise
- 1 tablespoon lime juice
- Salt and freshly ground black pepper
- ¼ medium head red cabbage, cored, halved, and very thinly sliced (about 4 cups)
- Kernels from 1 large ear of corn (about 1 cup)
- 1 large scallion, thinly sliced
- ¼ cup coarsely chopped fresh cilantro

BOWLS

- 1 batch cooked grains
- Roasted Red Pepper & Cashew Sauce (page 108)
- Toasted pepitas, for serving

Other Sauces to Try
- Creamy Chipotle Sauce (page 106)
- Smoky Red Pepper Sauce (page 61)

MOJO-MARINATED STEAK
WITH GRILLED VEGETABLES & ARUGULA + MOJO DRESSING

DRESSING

- ½ cup orange juice
- ½ cup lime juice
- 6 garlic cloves, minced
- ¾ teaspoon dried oregano
- ½ teaspoon ground cumin

  Salt and freshly ground black pepper
- ¼ cup extra-virgin olive oil

MAKE-AHEAD OPTION

The dressing can be refrigerated for up to 5 days.

This mojo dressing is a magical elixir, revitalizing vegetables, salads, and meats. I took inspiration from a Cuban mojo sauce, which is traditionally made with bitter oranges, olive oil, and loads of garlic. Since I can't find bitter oranges out here in the sticks, I use a combination of fresh orange and lime juice instead. Don't be intimidated by the amount of garlic — it mellows out in the dressing and is integral to the flavor.

The sliced steak is served with grilled vegetables (I go for scallions, asparagus, and red bell peppers, but you can use nearly any vegetable you like), along with spicy arugula, crumbled cotija or feta cheese, and plenty of dressing for drizzling (my mouth is watering just writing this!). You can also stuff everything into tacos.

For a vegetarian variation, swap out the steak for eggplant slices, portobello mushroom caps, or seitan, or simply increase the amount of grilled vegetables.

SERVES 4 | PREP TIME: 35 minutes | COOKING TIME: 25 minutes

MAKE THE DRESSING

1 Whisk together the orange juice, lime juice, garlic, oregano, and cumin in a small bowl. Season with salt and pepper to taste. Whisk in the oil.

BUILD THE BOWLS

2 Place the skirt steak in a ziplock plastic bag and add ¾ cup of the mojo dressing. Seal the bag and massage the contents to evenly coat the meat. Let sit at room temperature for 30 minutes, turning the bag occasionally.

3 Preheat a grill or grill pan to medium-high heat.

4 Toss the scallions, asparagus, and bell pepper separately with 1 teaspoon of the oil *each* and season with salt and black pepper. Arrange the vegetables on the grill (if your grill isn't big enough, do this in batches). Grill, turning the vegetables occasionally, until they are lightly charred and tender, 3 to 5 minutes for the scallions and asparagus and 6 to 8 minutes for the bell pepper. Transfer to a cutting board.

5 Remove the steak from the marinade and pat dry (discard the marinade). Season with salt and black pepper. Grill the steak until browned and caramelized on the bottom, 3 to 4 minutes. Flip and cook until browned on the other side, 3 to 4 minutes longer for medium-rare. Transfer to a cutting board and let rest for 5 to 10 minutes.

6 Coarsely chop the vegetables and thinly slice the meat against the grain.

7 Spoon the grains into bowls. Arrange the vegetables and steak in each bowl, along with a handful of arugula. Drizzle generously with mojo dressing. Sprinkle with crumbled cheese.

BOWLS

1 skirt steak (1–1½ pounds), cut crosswise into 3 or 4 pieces

1 bunch scallions

1 bunch asparagus (1 pound), tough ends trimmed

1 large red bell pepper, seeds and stem discarded, halved

3 teaspoons extra-virgin olive oil

Salt and freshly ground black pepper

1 batch cooked grains

Baby arugula, for serving

Crumbled cotija or feta cheese, for serving

143

GO AGAINST THE GRAIN

Skirt steak is my go-to cut of meat, because it cooks so quickly and has such a wonderful flavor. It's very tender, but you need to cut the meat against the grain for the best texture. That means you actually have to slice the steak vertically, not crosswise (you'll notice that the fibers of the meat run from side to side — you want to slice perpendicular to those fibers). Cutting the steak into three or four pieces before grilling makes it not only easier to handle on the grill but also easier to slice against the grain!

LAMB KOFTE
WITH SHAVED CARROT SALAD + GARLIC YOGURT

LAMB

- 1 pound ground lamb
- ¼ cup grated onion (grated on the large holes of a box grater)
- ½ cup finely chopped fresh mint
- ½ cup finely chopped fresh flat-leaf parsley
- 4 tablespoons toasted pine nuts, coarsely chopped
- 1 teaspoon ground cinnamon
- 1 teaspoon ground allspice

  Salt and freshly ground black pepper

SALAD

- 2 tablespoons lemon juice
- 1 teaspoon honey
- ¼ teaspoon ground cumin
- 3 tablespoons extra-virgin olive oil
- 3 large carrots

  Salt and freshly ground black pepper

BOWLS

- 1½ cups thawed frozen peas or cooked fresh peas
- 1 batch cooked grains

  Garlic Yogurt (page 99)

Other Sauces to Try

- Mint & Cilantro Sauce (page 146)
- Mint Pesto (page 65)
- Minty Yogurt (page 158)

Kofte is a minced meat kabob popular in Turkey and the Middle East, and it's one of the most delicious things ever. The meat is scented with mint, parsley, cinnamon, and allspice — formed into cigar shapes — and traditionally is grilled over a fire. In this simplified version, you sauté the meat instead. It is served over grains and sweet peas with a quick garlic yogurt sauce, which lends just the right amount of creaminess.

You can serve the kofte with nearly any vegetable, but I think you'll love this herby shaved carrot salad. To really take the meal over the top, serve the kofte over the Mujadarra on page 99 (they're also delicious stuffed into pita bread).

SERVES 4 | PREP TIME: 30 minutes | COOKING TIME: 20 minutes

MAKE THE LAMB

1 Combine the lamb, onion, ¼ cup of the mint, ¼ cup of the parsley, 2 tablespoons of the pine nuts, the cinnamon, and allspice in a large bowl. Season with salt and pepper. Using your hands or a fork, stir to evenly incorporate all of the ingredients. Shape the meat into eight 4- to 5-inch cigars. Let sit while you prep the salad.

MAKE THE SALAD

2 Whisk together the lemon juice, honey, and cumin, and season with salt and pepper in a large bowl. Slowly whisk in 2 tablespoons of the oil. Using a vegetable peeler, shave the carrots into long ribbons into the bowl (shave until the carrots get too thin or wobbly — save the rest for snacking). Toss to coat. Fold in the remaining ¼ cup mint, ¼ cup parsley, and 2 tablespoons pine nuts. Season with salt and pepper to taste.

3 Heat the remaining 1 tablespoon oil in a large skillet, preferably cast iron, over medium-high heat. Working in batches if needed, arrange the kofte in the pan in a single layer. Cook, turning occasionally (nudge them carefully with tongs), until browned on all sides but still pink in the middle, 6 to 9 minutes total (if the kofte are sticking, give them a few minutes longer to brown completely — they should loosen once browned). Transfer to a plate and let cool for 5 minutes.

BUILD THE BOWLS

4 Stir the peas into the grains.

5 Spoon the grains and peas into bowls. Arrange the kofte and the carrot salad over each and dollop with the garlic yogurt.

MOROCCAN-SPICED LAMB PATTIES
WITH ROASTED ZUCCHINI + MINT & CILANTRO SAUCE

SAUCE

- 1 garlic clove, peeled
- ½ small jalapeño, seeds and ribs discarded
- 1 cup lightly packed fresh cilantro leaves and tender stems
- 1 cup fresh mint leaves
- ¼ cup unsweetened shredded coconut
- ¼ teaspoon grated fresh gingerroot
- 1 tablespoon lime juice
- 1 teaspoon honey
- Salt and freshly ground black pepper
- 2 tablespoons water
- 6 tablespoons neutral vegetable oil (such as grapeseed)

Other Sauces to Try
- Mint Pesto (page 65)
- Minty Yogurt (page 158)
- Garlic Yogurt (page 99)

You're going to love the combination of these flavorful lamb patties with the vivid, slightly sweet cilantro sauce. While the patties take inspiration from the Moroccan pantry, I veered toward the Caribbean for the sauce, adding coconut and a touch of honey for sweetness. Garlicky roasted zucchini is an easy but crowd-pleasing accompaniment (I have to guard it like crown jewels or else half of it will get swiped from the pan before dinner starts).

The lamb also makes for killer burgers when shaped into four larger patties — serve them in buns with the sauce. Take note that you'll need mint for both the sauce and the patties.

SERVES 4 | PREP TIME: 30 minutes | COOKING TIME: 20 minutes

MAKE THE SAUCE

1 Drop the garlic clove and jalapeño into a food processor with the blade running. Add the cilantro, mint, coconut, gingerroot, lime juice, and honey, and season with salt and pepper. Process until a paste forms, scraping down the sides as needed. With the blade running, drizzle in the water, followed by the vegetable oil. Process until incorporated. Taste and season with additional salt and pepper as needed.

MAKE-AHEAD OPTIONS

The sauce can be refrigerated for up to 3 days. Place a piece of plastic wrap directly on the surface to help prevent it from browning.

The patties can be covered tightly with plastic wrap and refrigerated for up to 1 day.

BUILD THE BOWLS

2 Preheat the oven to 400°F (200°C). Line a baking sheet with aluminum foil.

3 Place the zucchini and half of the garlic in a large bowl and toss with 2 tablespoons of the olive oil. Season with salt and black pepper. Arrange the zucchini in a single layer on the baking sheet and bake for 15 minutes. Flip over each zucchini round and then bake for 5 minutes longer, or until tender. Remove the pan from the oven and sprinkle with 1 tablespoon of the mint.

4 In the meantime, place the lamb in a large bowl and add the remaining garlic, along with the shallot, gingerroot, coriander, Aleppo pepper, ground cloves, and the remaining 1 tablespoon mint. Season with salt and black pepper. Using your hands or a fork, stir to evenly incorporate all of the ingredients. Form 12 patties (they should be about 2 inches wide).

5 Heat the remaining 1 tablespoon olive oil in a large skillet over medium-high heat. Working in batches, sauté the lamb patties until browned on the bottom, 3 to 4 minutes. Flip the patties and cook until golden on the other side but still pink in the middle, 3 to 4 minutes longer (if needed, drain off the fat between batches).

6 Spoon the grains into bowls. Arrange the lamb patties and zucchini over the top and drizzle with the sauce. Top with sliced radishes and chopped pistachios.

BOWLS

2 medium zucchini (12 ounces), trimmed and sliced into ¼-inch-thick rounds

4 garlic cloves, minced

3 tablespoons extra-virgin olive oil

Salt and freshly ground black pepper

2 tablespoons finely chopped fresh mint

1 pound ground lamb

1 tablespoon minced shallot

1 teaspoon grated fresh gingerroot

1 teaspoon ground coriander

¼ teaspoon ground Aleppo pepper (or red pepper flakes)

Pinch of ground cloves

1 batch cooked rice or quinoa

Thinly sliced radishes, for serving

Coarsely chopped toasted pistachios, for serving

YOGURT-MARINATED LAMB KABOBS
WITH TOMATO, CUCUMBER & FETA SALAD

This meal has starred as our Easter supper several times, and it's one of my favorite ways to cook and eat leg of lamb. A robust yogurt marinade, which does double duty as a sauce for the kabobs, is seasoned with loads of fresh mint, along with toasted cumin and coriander seeds. It might seem like a pain to grind the spices, but it's worth it — it only takes a few minutes and the result is far more complex and aromatic than using purchased ground spices (plus, I love how toasted coriander seeds strangely smell like Fruity Pebbles cereal!).

The lamb will become even more flavorful the longer it sits. The sauce and salad are also delicious with vegetable kabobs, if you're feeding vegetarians. If you're using wooden skewers for the kabobs rather than metal ones, soak them in water for an hour or two first.

SERVES 4–6 | PREP TIME: 50 minutes | COOKING TIME: 10 minutes

MAKE THE MARINADE

1 Place the cumin and coriander seeds in a small skillet. Cook over medium heat, stirring occasionally, until fragrant, about 2 minutes. Coarsely grind the spices after they cool.

2 Combine the yogurt, ground spices, garlic, mint, Aleppo pepper, lemon juice, and oil in a large bowl. Season with salt and black pepper. Pour half of the yogurt sauce into a serving dish and refrigerate (this will be your sauce for later). Put the lamb in the bowl with the remaining sauce (this is your marinade — two birds with one stone!) and stir to coat. Let sit at room temperature for 30 minutes or in the refrigerator for up to 8 hours.

BUILD THE BOWLS

3 While the lamb marinates, combine the tomatoes, shallot, cucumber, feta, olives, mint, and oregano in a bowl.

4 Preheat a grill or grill pan to medium-high heat. Thread the lamb onto metal skewers (I put two skewers through each piece of meat so that the kabobs are easier to turn; otherwise the cubes tend to spin around). Season with salt and pepper.

5 Lightly oil the grill grates. Arrange the skewers on the grill in a single layer. Cook, flipping occasionally, until browned on all sides but still pink in the middle, 10 to 15 minutes total.

6 Finish the salad by tossing it with the lemon juice and oil. Season with salt and black pepper.

7 Spoon the grains into bowls. Arrange the lamb kabobs and salad over the top. Serve with the reserved yogurt sauce.

MARINADE

- 1 teaspoon cumin seeds
- 1 teaspoon coriander seeds
- 2 cups Greek yogurt (preferably 2% or whole-milk)
- 2 garlic cloves, grated on a Microplane or minced
- 3 tablespoons chopped fresh mint
- ¼ teaspoon ground Aleppo pepper or red pepper flakes
- 1 tablespoon lemon juice
- 2 teaspoons extra-virgin olive oil

  Salt and freshly ground black pepper
- 2 pounds boneless leg of lamb, trimmed of excess fat and cut into 1½-inch chunks

BOWLS

- 1 pint grape tomatoes, halved
- 1 small shallot, minced (rinse it in cold water if you prefer a milder taste)
- ½ medium English cucumber, finely diced
- ½ cup crumbled feta cheese
- ¼ cup kalamata olives, pitted and halved
- 1 tablespoon chopped fresh mint
- ¼ teaspoon dried oregano
- 1 tablespoon lemon juice
- 1 tablespoon extra-virgin olive oil
- 1 batch cooked grains

PAN-SEARED STEAK
WITH ROASTED VEGETABLES + SALSA VERDE

SALSA VERDE

- 1 garlic clove, peeled
- 1 anchovy fillet, rinsed and coarsely chopped
- 1 tablespoon coarsely chopped walnuts
- 1 teaspoon drained capers
- 1½ cups lightly packed fresh flat-leaf parsley leaves and tender stems
- 1 teaspoon chopped fresh thyme
- ½ teaspoon chopped fresh rosemary
- ½ teaspoon red wine vinegar or sherry vinegar

  Salt and freshly ground black pepper
- ½ cup extra-virgin olive oil

MAKE-AHEAD OPTIONS

The salsa verde can be refrigerated for up to 5 days. Bring to room temperature before serving.

Other Sauces to Try

- Classic Pesto (page 79)
- Sun-Dried Tomato Pesto (page 102)

This is one of my favorite Sunday suppers. I first tried salsa verde in Italy, and it instantly became one of my go-to ways to dress up a simple piece of meat or fish. The sauce packs a punch, so a little goes a long way, but trust me when I tell you that you'll want to drizzle it over everything. Don't be intimidated by the anchovy — it lends complexity, but you won't taste it.

Basting the steak with a small amount of browned butter at the end of cooking might sound luxurious, but it results in incredibly tender, juicy meat, particularly if you're using grass-fed steaks (which I prefer), because they're so lean. As far as the veggies go, feel free to swap in butternut squash, carrots, or broccoli. Start the vegetables first, then make the sauce while they cook. The steak and vegetables are also fabulous over polenta.

SERVES 4 | PREP TIME: 25 minutes | COOKING TIME: 30 minutes

MAKE THE SALSA VERDE

1 Drop the garlic clove into a food processor with the blade running. Add the anchovy, walnuts, capers, parsley, thyme, rosemary, and vinegar. Season with salt and pepper. Process until finely chopped, scraping the sides once or twice. With the blade running, slowly drizzle the olive oil through the feed tube to incorporate. Taste and season with additional salt and pepper, if needed.

BUILD THE BOWLS

2 Preheat the oven to 425°F (220°C). Line a baking sheet with aluminum foil.

3 Place the parsnips, sweet potato, and Brussels sprouts on the baking sheet and drizzle with the olive oil. Season with salt and pepper, and toss to coat. Spread the vegetables in a single layer. Roast, stirring once or twice, for 20 to 25 minutes, until the vegetables are browned and tender.

4 Let the steak (or steaks) sit at room temperature for 15 to 30 minutes. Pat dry and season generously with salt and pepper. Heat the vegetable oil in a large skillet, preferably cast iron, over medium-high heat. Once the oil is shimmering, add the steak. Cook until browned on the bottom, about 3 minutes. Flip and cook until browned on the other side, about 3 minutes longer. Prop the steak up on its edge and brown the sides, about 2 minutes. Lay the steak back in the pan and add the butter, thyme sprig, and rosemary sprig. Using a spoon, baste the steak with the melted butter, tilting the pan as needed to collect the butter. Keep basting, flipping the steak once, until it's cooked to your liking, about 2 to 4 minutes longer for medium-rare (the internal temperature should read 125 to 130°F/52 to 54°C for medium-rare). Transfer the steak to a cutting board and let rest for 10 minutes.

5 Thinly slice the steak against the grain.

6 Spoon the grains into bowls. Arrange the roasted vegetables and sliced steak in each bowl. Drizzle with the salsa verde.

BOWLS

2 medium parsnips, peeled and cut into ½-inch dice

1 medium sweet potato, peeled and cut into ½-inch dice

8 ounces Brussels sprouts, trimmed and halved (quartered if large)

2 tablespoons extra-virgin olive oil

Salt and freshly ground black pepper

1 pound sirloin or strip steak(s), 1–1½ inches thick

1 tablespoon neutral vegetable oil (such as grapeseed)

1 tablespoon unsalted butter

1 fresh thyme sprig

1 fresh rosemary sprig

1 batch cooked grains

TUNA NIÇOISE BOWLS + HERBY VINAIGRETTE, PAGE 169

SEAFOOD

A s a young girl in the Midwest, the only fish I ate was the frozen-in-a-box breaded variety. It wasn't until a fishmonger opened near our home when I was in high school that we had access to good-quality fresh salmon, sea bass, halibut, and other seafood. It was the start of a lifelong love affair. Seafood is now one of the foods (along with fruits, vegetables, and grains) that I could eat every single day and never tire of.

These simple but showstopping meals satisfy that desire without ever becoming boring, from crispy fish taco bowls that take me back to the beach (even if it's January) to ultra-easy but elegant roasted salmon bowls with herbed yogurt sauce to poke bowls that remind me of my honeymoon to steamed mussels that taste like France. Freshness is key when it comes to buying seafood — look for firm fish that smells like the sea.

CRISPY FISH TACO BOWLS WITH QUICK RED
CABBAGE & LIME SLAW + CREAMY CHIPOTLE SAUCE

SLAW

- 2 tablespoons lime juice
- 1 garlic clove, grated on a Microplane
- ½ jalapeño, seeded and minced
- ½ teaspoon ground cumin
- 2 tablespoons extra-virgin olive oil

  Salt and freshly ground black pepper
- ½ small red cabbage, very thinly sliced
- ¼ cup coarsely chopped fresh cilantro
- ¼ cup toasted pepitas

CRISPY FISH

- ½ cup corn flour or all-purpose flour
- 2 eggs, beaten
- 1 cup panko breadcrumbs (regular or gluten-free)

  Salt and freshly ground black pepper

  Cayenne pepper
- 1 pound skinless cod or hake, cut into 2-inch chunks

  Neutral vegetable oil (such as grapeseed), for frying

BOWLS

- 1 batch cooked grains
- 1 avocado, pitted, peeled, and thinly sliced

  Creamy Chipotle Sauce (page 106)

  Lime wedges, for serving

  Hot sauce, for serving

Let's take a trip to the beach, shall we? These crispy fish taco bowls will bring the ocean to your doorstep, even if you're as landlocked as Nebraska. Chunks of white fish are breaded and then panfried until golden and crisp. They are served with a quick red cabbage and lime slaw and drizzled with a sweet and spicy chipotle sauce, which is one of my very favorite sauces (try it with the Roasted Cauliflower & Squash bowls on page 106). The combination of the warm fish, cool slaw, and spicy sauce is pure nirvana.

This is one of my favorite meals in the summer, eaten out on the deck, and it's also pretty great in the dead of winter, when I'm dreaming of warmer weather. Grab your swimsuit — or spatula, that is — and cook yourself away to warmer climes.

SERVES 4 | PREP TIME: 35 minutes | COOKING TIME: 10 minutes

MAKE THE SLAW

1 Place the lime juice, garlic, jalapeño, and cumin in a large bowl and whisk in the olive oil. Season with salt and pepper to taste. Add the red cabbage, cilantro, and pepitas, and season with more salt and pepper. Toss to coat. Taste and adjust the seasonings as needed.

BUILD THE BOWLS

2 Set up a dredging station with the corn flour, whisked eggs, and panko in separate shallow bowls. Season each bowl with salt and black pepper, and add a pinch (or two, if you like it spicy!) of cayenne to the flour and panko.

3 Season the fish with salt and black pepper. Working in batches, dredge the fish in the flour on all sides, followed by the eggs and then the panko. Transfer the breaded fish to waxed paper or parchment paper while you heat up your skillet.

4 Heat ¼ inch of vegetable oil in a large cast-iron or nonstick skillet over medium-high heat until shimmering (you can add a pinch of panko to test if the oil is hot enough — the panko should immediately start to sizzle). Working in batches, fry the fish until golden brown on both sides and cooked through, 2 to 3 minutes per side (it should flake easily when cut and be white throughout). Transfer to paper towels to drain and sprinkle with salt.

5 Spoon the grains into bowls. Arrange the slaw and crispy fish over the top, along with a few avocado slices. Drizzle with the creamy chipotle sauce and serve with lime wedges and hot sauce.

Other Sauces to Try
- Guacamole (page 115) • Roasted Red Pepper & Cashew Sauce (page 108)

ROASTED SHRIMP WITH SNOW PEAS & SWEET CORN
+ MINT & CILANTRO SAUCE

The first time I made this recipe, there was silence at the table. If you were to meet my giggling (read: shrieking) kids, you would understand how strange this was. To my surprise, rather than the silent protest I was expecting, the girls were instead utterly absorbed in their food. The roasted shrimp, which are flavored with garlic, gingerroot, and lime zest, are seriously addicting on their own but are made even better with the mint and cilantro sauce, which has a touch of sweetness from coconut and honey.

You can swap out the corn and snow peas for other seasonal vegetables, such as roasted squash, zucchini, lightly dressed cabbage, or sautéed greens. These bowls are especially beautiful with black rice, but any grain will do.

SERVES 4 | PREP TIME: 30 minutes | COOKING TIME: 15 minutes

1 Preheat the oven to 400°F (200°C). Line a baking sheet with aluminum foil.

2 Pat the shrimp dry using paper towels and transfer to the baking sheet. Sprinkle with the garlic, gingerroot, and lime zest, and season with salt and pepper. Drizzle with the oil and toss to coat. Spread the shrimp in a single layer.

3 Roast for 6 to 10 minutes, stirring once or twice, until pink and cooked through (the cooking time will depend on the size of the shrimp).

4 In the meantime, fill a medium pot with about 1 inch of water and insert a steamer basket. Bring the water to a simmer. Add the corn and cover. Cook until bright yellow and tender crisp, 5 to 8 minutes. Transfer to a plate (don't drain the pot). Rub the corn with butter and season with salt. Place the snow peas in the steamer. Cover and cook until bright green and tender crisp, about 2 minutes. Drain and rinse under cold water to stop the cooking. Slice the peas on the diagonal.

5 Spoon the grains into bowls. Arrange the shrimp, snow peas, and corn in each bowl. Spoon the mint and cilantro sauce over the top.

1 pound peeled and deveined shrimp

1 large garlic clove, minced

1 teaspoon minced fresh gingerroot

½ teaspoon lime zest

Salt and freshly ground black pepper

1 tablespoon neutral vegetable oil (such as grapeseed)

2 ears of corn, husked, cobs broken in half

Unsalted butter or virgin coconut oil, for the corn

2 cups (6 ounces) snow peas

1 batch cooked grains, preferably black rice

Mint & Cilantro Sauce (page 146)

Other Sauces to Try
- Roasted Red Pepper & Cashew Sauce (page 108)
- Coconut-Peanut Sauce (page 119)

ROASTED SALMON & ASPARAGUS
+ HERBED YOGURT SAUCE

This is the meal I make every year when asparagus first appears at the farmers' market. It's super-simple and fast but sophisticated enough for dinner with friends. Roasted wild salmon and asparagus are served on a bed of grains with a quick yogurt sauce that's enlivened with fresh herbs and capers. I prefer to use whole-milk yogurt for the sauce — if you go for low-fat, whisk in a touch of olive oil to round out the flavor. The bowls are topped with paper-thin slices of peppery radishes and a small scatter of greens. Oh spring, how I've missed you.

SERVES 4 | **PREP TIME:** 10 minutes | **COOKING TIME:** 10 minutes

MAKE THE SAUCE

1 Combine the lemon juice and garlic in a small bowl. Let sit for 5 minutes (this will mellow out the garlic). Add the yogurt, capers, dill, chives, and tarragon, and season with salt and pepper to taste. Stir to combine.

BUILD THE BOWLS

2 Preheat the oven to 425°F (220°C). Line two baking sheets with aluminum foil.

3 Place the salmon on one of the baking sheets and drizzle with 1 teaspoon of the oil. Season with salt and pepper.

4 Place the asparagus on the second baking sheet and drizzle with the remaining 2 teaspoons oil. Season with salt and pepper, and toss to coat.

5 Roast the salmon and asparagus for 8 to 15 minutes, until the salmon flakes easily with a fork (it should still be pink in the middle) and the asparagus is bright green and tender. (The cooking time will depend on the thickness of the salmon and asparagus — feel free to pull one or the other out earlier, if needed.) Let cool for 5 minutes. Using a fork, flake the salmon into large pieces (discard the skin).

6 In the meantime, place the radishes in a small bowl of ice water (this will help crisp them up). Let sit for 10 minutes. Drain.

7 Spoon the grains into bowls. Arrange the salmon and asparagus over the top, along with a small pile of microgreens. Season with salt and pepper to taste. Drizzle with the yogurt sauce and top with the radishes. Serve with additional yogurt sauce on the side.

HERBED YOGURT SAUCE

- 1 teaspoon lemon juice
- 1 garlic clove, grated on a Microplane
- 1¼ cups plain yogurt (preferably whole-milk)
- 1 tablespoon drained capers
- 1 tablespoon chopped fresh dill
- 1 tablespoon thinly sliced fresh chives
- 1 teaspoon chopped fresh tarragon

  Salt and freshly ground black pepper

BOWLS

- 1 pound skin-on wild salmon
- 3 teaspoons extra-virgin olive oil

  Salt and freshly ground black pepper
- 1 pound asparagus, tough ends trimmed
- 3 medium radishes, very thinly sliced
- 1 batch cooked grains

  Microgreens, watercress, or baby arugula, for serving

Other Sauces to Try
- Chive Crème Fraîche (page 58)
- Mint Pesto (page 65)
- Classic Pesto (page 79)
- Minty Yogurt (page 158)
- Salsa Verde (page 150)
- Pistachio-Yogurt Sauce (page 166)

CURRY-ROASTED SALMON
WITH TOMATO-BRAISED CHICKPEAS + MINTY YOGURT

MINTY YOGURT SAUCE

- 1 teaspoon lemon juice
- 1 small garlic clove, grated on a Microplane
- 1 cup plain Greek yogurt (preferably 2% or whole-milk)
- 1 teaspoon extra-virgin olive oil
- 2 tablespoons coarsely chopped fresh mint
- 2 tablespoons coarsely chopped fresh cilantro

  Salt and freshly ground black pepper

MAKE-AHEAD OPTION

The sauce can be refrigerated for up to 1 day.

Other Sauces to Try
- Garlic Yogurt (page 99)

When it comes to weeknight cooking, roasted salmon is one of my staples. It takes very little effort but feels elegant, turning an average Tuesday into something special. Here salmon is dusted with curry powder and brown sugar before going into the oven, and it is served over a quick tomato, chickpea, and spinach curry. A dollop of minty yogurt sauce complements the fish and chills out the spice.

This meal is fancy enough for a dinner party but easy enough to knock out after a long day at work. You can also do a similar preparation using chicken breasts: dust the breasts with curry powder; sauté them in olive oil; slice them thinly (against the grain); and fan the slices over the chickpeas with a dollop of yogurt on top.

For a vegetarian variation, omit the salmon and double the quantities for the tomato-braised chickpeas.

SERVES 4 | PREP TIME: 10 minutes | COOKING TIME: 25 minutes

MAKE THE SAUCE

1 Combine the lemon juice and garlic in a small bowl. Let sit for 5 minutes (this will mellow out the garlic). Add the yogurt, oil, mint, and cilantro, and season with salt and pepper. Taste and add additional lemon juice or olive oil as needed, depending on the tartness of the yogurt.

BUILD THE BOWLS

2 Preheat the oven to 425°F (220°C). Line a baking sheet with parchment paper.

3 Pour the oil into a large skillet and add the garlic. Cook over medium heat, stirring, until the garlic is fragrant but not browned, 1 to 2 minutes. Sprinkle in 1½ teaspoons of the curry powder and cook for 30 seconds. Pile in the spinach and season with salt and pepper. Cook, stirring, until the spinach is mostly wilted. Add the chickpeas, tomatoes (with their juices), and ⅛ teaspoon of the sugar. Bring to a simmer and cook until slightly thickened, 10 to 15 minutes. Add the lemon juice and season with salt and pepper as needed.

4 In the meantime, mix the remaining ½ teaspoon curry powder with the remaining ½ teaspoon sugar. Place the salmon fillets on the baking sheet, skin side down. Season the fish with salt and pepper, and sprinkle with the curry powder mixture. Use your fingers to rub the seasonings evenly over the flesh of the fish. Roast the salmon until the fish flakes easily with a fork but is still slightly pink in the middle, 8 to 15 minutes.

5 Spoon the grains into bowls, followed by the tomato-braised chickpeas. Using a spatula, transfer a piece of fish to each bowl, leaving the fish skin behind. Top with a dollop of the minty yogurt. Serve with additional yogurt sauce at the table.

BOWLS

2 tablespoons extra-virgin olive oil

2 garlic cloves, minced

2 teaspoons curry powder

5 ounces baby spinach

Salt and freshly ground black pepper

1 (15-ounce) can chickpeas, rinsed and drained

1 (14-ounce) can diced or whole baby Roma tomatoes

½ teaspoon plus ⅛ teaspoon packed brown sugar

1 teaspoon lemon juice

4 (6-ounce) skin-on wild salmon fillets

1 batch cooked grains

STEAMED MUSSELS
WITH FENNEL, WHITE WINE & TOMATOES

I was first introduced to mussels in their shells, fish stews, and fennel while studying in the south of France during college, and I've had a love affair with the region and its foods ever since. This dish therefore has my heart. Fennel, sweet onion, and garlic are layered with white wine, chicken broth, or fish stock (opt for chicken broth unless you can find good-quality fresh or frozen fish stock — your local fishmonger is a good source), tomatoes, hearty grains, and mussels. The mussels and grains soak up all the delicious sauce.

Serve this with a crisp glass of white wine and a toasty baguette for mopping up your bowl, and let yourself be transported to France.

SERVES 4 | PREP TIME: 10 minutes | COOKING TIME: 10 minutes

1 Heat the oil in a large Dutch oven over medium heat. Add the onion, fennel, and garlic. Season with salt and black pepper. Cook, stirring occasionally, until the vegetables are softened and light golden, 5 to 7 minutes. Add the saffron and pepper flakes, and cook, stirring, for 30 seconds. Add the tomatoes and wine, and bring to a boil. Stir in the chicken broth and grains. Increase the heat to high and return to a boil.

2 Add the mussels and stir to coat. Cover and cook for 1 minute, then stir. Cover and continue cooking, checking after each minute, until the mussels have opened, 3 to 5 minutes total. Discard any mussels that didn't open. Remove the pot from the heat and season with salt and black pepper. Stir in the tarragon and parsley.

3 Divide the mussels and sauce among bowls. Serve with lemon wedges and crusty bread, if desired.

BROTH

- 3 tablespoons extra-virgin olive oil
- 1 medium sweet onion, thinly sliced
- 1 medium fennel bulb, trimmed, halved, and thinly sliced
- 4 large garlic cloves, thinly sliced
- Salt and freshly ground black pepper
- Pinch of saffron
- Pinch of red pepper flakes
- 2 plum tomatoes, seeded and diced
- ½ cup white wine
- 1 cup low-sodium chicken broth or good-quality fish stock
- 2 cups cooked sorghum, wheat berries, spelt berries, Khorasan wheat (Kamut), farro, or einkorn

MUSSELS

- 2 pounds mussels, scrubbed well and debearded (see box, left)
- Salt and freshly ground black pepper
- 2 tablespoons finely chopped fresh tarragon
- 2 tablespoons finely chopped fresh flat-leaf parsley
- Lemon wedges, for serving
- Crusty bread for serving (optional)

CLEANING & DEBEARDING MUSSELS

With their sweet, meaty flavor, mussels are probably my favorite shellfish, and they're really easy to prep at home. First, rinse them well in cold water, brushing off any seaweed or mud (if they're farm-raised, they will most likely already be pretty clean). If your mussels still have their beards attached, which look like thin sticky membranes or hairs coming out of their shells, pull those off. Now you're ready to cook!

BROILED SEA BASS & EGGPLANT
+ MAPLE-MISO GLAZE

MAPLE-MISO GLAZE

- ¼ cup mirin
- ¼ cup sake
- ¼ cup white miso
- 1½ tablespoons maple syrup
- 1 tablespoon low-sodium tamari or soy sauce
- 1 teaspoon grated fresh gingerroot

This glaze, made with miso paste, maple syrup, mirin, sake, and gingerroot, is pure magic. It transforms sea bass and roasted eggplant into sweet and savory masterpieces, with an indescribable but subtle umami flavor that I literally *crave*. The caramelized fish and eggplant are served over grains (I prefer rice or quinoa), along with spicy watercress, a sprinkle of scallions and basil, and a drizzle of toasted sesame oil.

It's a meal that feels utterly indulgent while being downright healthy. Mirin is a sweet Japanese rice wine that can be found at most grocery stores in the Asian section. I prefer these bowls with white rice.

SERVES 4 | PREP TIME: 30 minutes | COOKING TIME: 30 minutes

MAKE THE GLAZE

1 Whisk together the mirin, sake, miso, maple syrup, tamari, and gingerroot in a small bowl until smooth.

MISO

There are several different types of miso, categorized by color, with white, yellow, and red being the most common. White miso (which actually looks light yellow) is the mildest, with a slightly sweet flavor. Use it in the miso butter on page 52, whisk it into salad dressings, or add it to marinades and sauces.

BUILD THE BOWLS

2 Preheat the oven to 425°F (220°C). Line a large baking sheet with aluminum foil and brush it with olive oil. Line another baking sheet with aluminum foil.

3 Measure out ¼ cup of the miso glaze and set it aside. Place the sea bass in a bowl and pour the remaining glaze over the top. Turn the fish to coat. Cover and refrigerate for 30 minutes, turning the fish once or twice.

4 Trim off the ends of the eggplants, then cut them in half lengthwise. Season the cut halves of the eggplant with salt and let sit for 10 minutes.

5 Blot the eggplants dry with paper towels, then place them cut sides down on the oil-brushed baking sheet. Roast for 15 to 20 minutes, until the skin is slightly shriveled and the flesh is tender. Remove the pan from the oven and preheat the broiler.

6 Turn the eggplants over so that the cut side is facing up. Brush them generously with the reserved glaze. Broil the eggplants about 2 inches from the heat source for 2 to 4 minutes, until the glaze is bubbling and the eggplants are golden brown on top, turning the pan halfway through. Remove the pan from the oven and set aside (keep the broiler on).

7 Remove the fish from the marinade, reserving the marinade. Place the fish on the foil-lined baking sheet and broil about 2 inches from the heat source for about 4 minutes, or until browned on the edges. Carefully flip the fish over, brush it with some marinade from the bowl, and broil for 3 to 4 minutes longer, until browned on the other side and cooked through.

8 Toss the watercress with the sesame oil and lime juice in a large bowl. Season with salt to taste.

9 Spoon the grains into bowls. Arrange the eggplant, sea bass, and watercress over each bowl. Drizzle the bowls with a touch more sesame oil, then top with the scallions and basil. Sprinkle with sesame seeds, if using.

BOWLS

4 (6-ounce) skinless sea bass fillets, ¾ to 1 inch thick

2 long Japanese eggplants or 3 or 4 small Italian eggplants (1 pound total)

Salt

Olive oil, for brushing

2 cups watercress or microgreens

½ teaspoon toasted sesame oil, plus more for serving

Juice of ½ lime

1 batch cooked rice or quinoa

2 tablespoons thinly sliced scallions

2 tablespoons chopped fresh basil

Toasted sesame seeds, for serving (optional)

MAKE-AHEAD OPTIONS

The glaze can be refrigerated for up to 3 days.

The sea bass can be marinated for up to 4 hours; turn it occasionally.

POKE BOWLS

POKE

- 1 pound sushi-grade tuna or wild salmon, skinned and cut into ½-inch cubes
- ½ cup finely diced sweet yellow onion, rinsed in cold water and drained well
- 1 scallion, thinly sliced
- 2 tablespoons low-sodium tamari or soy sauce
- 2 teaspoons toasted sesame oil
- 1 teaspoon honey
- 1 teaspoon sriracha
- 1 tablespoon toasted sesame seeds, plus more for serving

  Salt and freshly ground black pepper

- 1 small avocado, pitted, peeled, and diced

BOWLS

- 1 batch cooked white or brown rice
- 1 cup baby spinach
- 2 teaspoons rice vinegar
- 1 teaspoon neutral vegetable oil (such as grapeseed)

  Sliced cucumbers, for serving

  Roasted seaweed snack sheets, torn into bite-size pieces, for serving (optional)

Poke is a raw fish salad from Hawaii, usually eaten as an appetizer or roadside snack over rice or with tortilla chips for scooping. It's now gone mainstream on the mainland, where you can find it on restaurant menus and even in some grocery stores. I love making it at home because (a) it's easy and fast; (b) it's freaking delicious; and (c) it takes me back to my honeymoon in Hawaii more than a dozen years ago — cue the starry eyes.

I think this version will give *you* starry eyes, even if you've never been to the islands (or married my husband). Sushi-grade tuna or fresh wild salmon (buy the freshest you can get) is mixed with a quick tamari dressing and avocado and is served over warm rice with spinach. Pull out your chopsticks, and let me tell you the story about how we lost — and then miraculously found — James's wedding ring on the beach. . . .

SERVES 4 | PREP TIME: 15 minutes

1 Place the tuna in a large bowl and add the onion, scallion, tamari, sesame oil, honey, sriracha, and sesame seeds. Season with salt and pepper, and stir gently to combine. Fold in the avocado. Taste and season with more salt, pepper, or tamari, if needed.

2 Reheat the rice, if needed (you want it warm, so that the spinach will wilt slightly). Stir in the spinach, along with the vinegar and vegetable oil.

3 Spoon the rice into bowls and top with the poke. Top with sliced cucumbers and a few roasted seaweed snack sheets, if using. Sprinkle with sesame seeds.

ROASTED SEAWEED SNACKS

Roasted seaweed snack sheets can now be found in most supermarkets, usually in the Asian section or with the snack foods and chips (they're packaged like crackers). They're small, thin sheets of seaweed that have been roasted with oil and salt, resulting in a savory and surprisingly addicting flavor and texture. They're a healthy snack that even my kids love!

ROASTED WHITE FISH & CARAMELIZED CARROTS + PISTACHIO-YOGURT SAUCE

PISTACHIO-YOGURT SAUCE

- 1 garlic clove, peeled
- ¼ cup toasted unsalted pistachios
- 1 tablespoon lemon juice
- 2 teaspoons olive oil
- 1 cup whole-milk plain yogurt

  Salt and freshly ground black pepper

MAKE-AHEAD OPTION

The yogurt sauce can be refrigerated for up to 1 day.

Other Sauces to Try

- Minty Yogurt (page 158)
- Garlic Yogurt (page 99)
- Mint & Cilantro Sauce (page 146)

While this roasted white fish slathered with a quick coriander- and cumin-spiked spice rub is a stunner on its own, the addition of a pistachio-yogurt sauce, caramelized carrots, and a pickled shallot and parsley salad take it from festive cocktail attire to dashing black tie (meaning I get to feel like a fashion stylist, even if it's just for a piece of fish).

While toasting whole spices might seem like a tedious step, trust me when I tell you it's worth it, resulting in a much fruitier flavor profile. I use an electric coffee grinder or small mortar and pestle to grind the spices, but in a pinch you can smash them with a rolling pin (it's okay if they're rather coarse).

SERVES 4 | PREP TIME: 20 minutes | COOKING TIME: 25 minutes

MAKE THE SAUCE

1 Chop the garlic clove by dropping it in the food processor with the blade running. Add the pistachios and process until the nuts are finely chopped. Add the lemon juice and oil, and pulse to combine. The nuts should look sticky along the side of the bowl, but there should still be some slightly bigger pieces.

2 Place the yogurt in a bowl and stir in the pistachio paste. Season with salt and pepper to taste.

BUILD THE BOWLS

3 Preheat the oven to 450°F (230°C) with racks in the lower third and upper third of the oven. Line one baking sheet with aluminum foil and another baking sheet with parchment paper.

4 Mix the shallot with the vinegar in a small bowl (it's okay if the vinegar doesn't completely cover the shallots). Let sit while you prep the other ingredients, stirring it now and then.

5 Toss the carrots with 1 tablespoon of the oil in a bowl and season with salt and pepper. Spread the carrots in a single layer on the foil-lined baking sheet.

6 Place the cumin and coriander seeds in a small skillet. Cook over medium heat, stirring occasionally, until fragrant, about 2 minutes. Transfer to a mortar and pestle or spice grinder (I use an old coffee grinder) and let cool. Coarsely grind the spices. Transfer the spices to a small bowl and add the chopped parsley, cilantro, and 1 tablespoon of the oil. Sprinkle the fish fillets with salt and pepper on both sides, then rub them with the herb mixture. Arrange the fish on the parchment-lined baking sheet and top each fillet with 2 or 3 lemon slices.

7 Place the carrots on the lower rack of the oven and set a timer for 10 minutes. When the timer goes off, stir the carrots and slide the fish onto the upper rack. Roast for 10 to 15 minutes longer, until the carrots are lightly browned and the fish is opaque throughout and flakes easily (if needed, remove the carrots or fish earlier).

8 Drain the shallots, reserving the vinegar. Toss the shallots with the parsley leaves, the remaining 1 teaspoon oil, and 1 teaspoon of the reserved vinegar. Season with salt and pepper to taste.

9 Spoon the grains into bowls. Arrange the fish and carrots over the top, along with a spoonful of the pistachio-yogurt sauce. Top with the parsley salad.

BOWLS

1 small shallot, very thinly sliced

2 tablespoons sherry vinegar

1 pound carrots (6–8 medium carrots), sliced ¼ inch thick

2 tablespoons plus 1 teaspoon olive oil

Salt and freshly ground black pepper

1 teaspoon cumin seeds

1 teaspoon coriander seeds

1 tablespoon finely chopped fresh flat-leaf parsley plus ½ cup lightly packed leaves

1 tablespoon finely chopped fresh cilantro

4 (6-ounce) fillets firm white fish (such as striped bass or halibut), preferably ¾ to 1 inch thick

1 lemon, very thinly sliced

1 batch cooked grains

WHY LINE-CAUGHT TUNA?

Most tuna is caught with huge nets, which scoop up and kill everything they grab (including turtles, sharks, and even small whales). Line-caught tuna is caught using a fishing line, meaning there's no bycatch. It's a much more sustainable option that helps to prevent overfishing as well as to preserve certain species. I recommend Wild Planet and American Tuna brands, which both source younger, smaller wild tuna that have accumulated lower levels of mercury compared to larger tuna. These brands are also packed without water and therefore have a meaty texture and flavor.

TUNA NIÇOISE BOWLS
+ HERBY VINAIGRETTE

Unlike a tossed salad, a Niçoise salad is composed, meaning each element is dressed separately and then piled onto the plate in little bundles. My version is loaded with green beans, tomatoes, cucumbers, canned tuna, olives, artichoke hearts, thinly sliced radishes, and hard-boiled eggs. Instead of the more traditional roasted potatoes, whole grains soak up all the dressing.

Speaking of which, the dressing is packed with fresh herbs (feel free to use what you have on hand) as well as a few anchovies for salty complexity — as with Caesar dressing, they're optional. Feel free to swap out the canned tuna for cooked salmon, shrimp, or seared fresh tuna.

For a vegetarian variation, omit the anchovies in the dressing and swap out the tuna for white beans.

SERVES 4 | PREP TIME: 25 minutes | COOKING TIME: 10–15 minutes

MAKE THE VINAIGRETTE

1 Whisk together the lemon juice, vinegar, mustard, garlic, shallot, anchovies (if using), capers, basil, thyme, and tarragon in a small bowl. Season with salt and pepper to taste. Slowly whisk in the oil.

BUILD THE BOWLS

2 Peel and halve or quarter the eggs, if using.

3 Fill a medium pot with about 1 inch of water and insert a steamer basket. Bring the water to a simmer. Add the green beans and cover. Cook until the beans are bright green and tender crisp, 4 to 6 minutes. Drain and rinse under cold water to stop the cooking. Pat dry. Transfer to a bowl and toss with about 2 tablespoons of the dressing. Season with salt and pepper to taste.

4 Spoon the grains into bowls and arrange the green beans alongside (I like to mound them in separate piles). Put the tomatoes in the same bowl you used for the green beans and toss with about 1 tablespoon of the dressing. Season with salt and pepper to taste, and toss to coat. Pile the tomatoes into the serving bowls. Put the cucumbers in the same bowl and toss with about 1 tablespoon of the dressing. Pile the cucumbers into the serving bowls. Arrange the tuna in the bowls and drizzle it with some of the dressing. Top each bowl with the artichoke hearts, olives, eggs, and radishes. Drizzle everything with a bit more dressing and serve with any additional dressing on the side.

VINAIGRETTE

- 2 tablespoons lemon juice
- 2 tablespoons red wine vinegar
- 2 teaspoons Dijon mustard
- 1 garlic clove, minced
- ½ small shallot, minced (about 1 tablespoon)
- 2 anchovies, rinsed and finely chopped (optional)
- 1 tablespoon drained capers
- 1 tablespoon finely chopped fresh basil
- 1 teaspoon finely chopped fresh thyme
- 1 teaspoon finely chopped fresh tarragon
- Salt and freshly ground black pepper
- ¼ cup extra-virgin olive oil

BOWLS

- 4 eggs, hard- or soft-boiled (optional)
- 8 ounces green beans
- Salt and freshly ground black pepper
- ½ batch cooked grains (cooled)
- 1½ cups halved grape tomatoes or chopped heirloom tomatoes
- 1½ cups diced cucumber
- 10 ounces line-caught canned tuna
- 4 canned or jarred whole artichoke hearts, quartered
- Pitted kalamata olives, for serving
- Thinly sliced radishes, for serving

SLOW-ROASTED COD
+ TOMATO & BLACK OLIVE SALSA

SALSA

- 1 tablespoon minced shallot
- 1 pint grape or cherry tomatoes, halved or quartered
- ½ cup pitted kalamata olives, halved
- 1 tablespoon drained capers
- 1 garlic clove, grated on a Microplane
- ½ teaspoon lemon zest
- 1 tablespoon fresh lemon juice
- ¼ cup coarsely chopped fresh parsley
- ½ teaspoon minced fresh oregano
- 2 tablespoons extra-virgin olive oil
- Sea salt and freshly ground black pepper

BOWLS

- 4 (6-ounce) skinned cod or hake fillets (1½ pounds total)
- Salt and freshly ground black pepper
- 1 garlic clove, grated on a Microplane
- ½ teaspoon minced fresh oregano
- 1 teaspoon minced fresh parsley
- 2 tablespoons fresh lemon juice
- 2 tablespoons extra-virgin olive oil
- 1 batch cooked grains

If you're looking for an easy and fail-proof fish recipe, this is your dish. Roasting fresh cod at a really low temperature results in perfectly moist and flaky fish that's nearly impossible to overcook. A juicy, salty-sweet tomato and olive salsa gives the mild fish a punch of bright flavor (sometimes I'll add a chopped anchovy or two to the salsa for an even bigger wallop). Serve the fish and salsa over whole grains for a light but elegant meal.

SERVES 4 | PREP TIME: 20 minutes | COOKING TIME: 20–30 minutes

MAKE THE SALSA

1 Rinse the shallot in a small strainer to remove the onion-y "bite" (if you don't mind the bite, feel free to skip this step). Combine the shallot, tomatoes, olives, capers, garlic, lemon zest, lemon juice, parsley, oregano, and oil in a medium bowl. Season with sea salt and pepper. Let sit for 10 minutes (or up to an hour) at room temperature to allow the flavors to meld.

BUILD THE BOWLS

2 Preheat the oven to 275°F (135°C). Arrange the fish fillets in an oven-proof dish and season with salt and pepper.

3 Combine the garlic, oregano, parsley, lemon juice, and oil in a small bowl. Spoon the mixture over the fish, spreading it around to evenly coat. Bake for 20 to 30 minutes, until the fish is white all the way through and flakes easily with a fork.

4 Spoon the grains into bowls. Top each bowl with a fillet of fish and a generous helping of salsa.

SPICY COCONUT SHRIMP
WITH KALE & CILANTRO

If food could be sexy, I'd call this dish Jessica Rabbit. There's something about the spicy coconut sauce, sweet shrimp, and tangle of garlicky kale that feels downright sultry. I developed the recipe for my website a couple of years ago, and it's still one of my very favorite meals, especially when enjoyed on a date-night-in with my husband (even if the kids are just playing in the next room).

Best of all, it uses only one skillet. First, you cook kale with onions and garlic, then you use the same pan to sauté shrimp and build a two-minute coconut milk and sriracha sauce. I prefer to serve this over white rice, which soaks up all that delicious sauce while letting the flavors shine. If you don't have a lid for your skillet, cover it with a large baking sheet.

SERVES 4 | PREP TIME: 15 minutes | COOKING TIME: 20 minutes

MAKE THE KALE

1 Melt the butter in a large skillet over medium heat. Add the onion and half of the garlic. Season with salt and pepper. Cook, stirring often, until the onion is softened and starting to brown, 3 to 4 minutes.

2 Add the kale and season with a bit more salt and pepper. Pour in 2 tablespoons of water. Cover and cook, stirring occasionally, until the kale is wilted and tender, 7 to 10 minutes. Add more water as needed if the skillet starts to look dry. Stir in the lemon juice. Taste and season with additional salt, pepper, or lemon juice, if needed. Transfer to a bowl and cover to keep warm.

MAKE THE SHRIMP

3 Wipe the skillet clean and place it back over medium heat. Add the butter. Once melted, add the sriracha and the remaining garlic; cook, stirring, for 1 minute. Add the shrimp and season with salt and pepper. Cook, stirring occasionally, until the shrimp are almost cooked through but still pink in the middle, 2 to 4 minutes, depending on the size of your shrimp. Transfer the shrimp to a plate.

4 Place the skillet back over medium heat (don't wash it) and add the coconut milk and sugar. Bring to a boil and cook, stirring, until slightly thickened around the edges, about 1 minute. Scrape the shrimp and any juices back into the skillet and simmer until the shrimp are cooked through. Remove the pan from the heat and season with additional salt, pepper, and/or sriracha, as desired. Stir in the cilantro and scallions.

5 Spoon the rice into bowls. Top with the kale, then spoon the shrimp and sauce over the top. Sprinkle with more cilantro and scallions.

KALE

- 2 tablespoons unsalted butter
- ½ medium red onion, thinly sliced
- 4 large garlic cloves, thinly sliced

  Salt and freshly ground black pepper
- 1 bunch curly kale, stems discarded, leaves coarsely chopped (about 8 cups chopped)
- 2 tablespoons water, plus more as needed

  Juice of ½ lemon, plus more as needed

SHRIMP

- 2 tablespoons unsalted butter
- 3 tablespoons sriracha, plus more as needed
- 1 pound shelled and deveined shrimp

  Salt and freshly ground black pepper
- 1 cup full-fat coconut milk (well stirred)
- ¼ teaspoon sugar
- 1 tablespoon finely chopped fresh cilantro, plus more for serving
- 1 tablespoon thinly sliced scallions, plus more for serving
- 1 batch cooked rice

ACKNOWLEDGMENTS

I'd like to thank Ella and Juniper, who are my life's joy (and my harshest critics). Thank you for being such wonderful teachers, and for showing me that meals are best ended with dance parties.

James, for being my ultimate taste tester, champion, and partner. You have no idea how much I love the fact that you say "thank you" every single night for dinner, even when it doesn't turn out quite right.

My editors and collaborators at Storey Publishing, who have been so welcoming and supportive. It's been a true joy working with you.

Mom and Dad. Tina and Mike. For being the best cheerleaders (and parents) ever.

My friends and family (you know who you are). I am blessed to have such an incredible support system.

And finally, thank you to my From Scratch Fast readers, who continuously inspire me and fuel me to do more. This one's for you.

METRIC CONVERSION CHARTS

Unless you have finely calibrated measuring equipment, conversions between US and metric measurements will be somewhat inexact. It's important to convert the measurements for all of the ingredients in a recipe to maintain the same proportions as the original.

WEIGHT

TO CONVERT	TO	MULTIPLY
ounces	grams	ounces by 28.35
pounds	grams	pounds by 453.5
pounds	kilograms	pounds by 0.45

US	METRIC
0.035 ounce	1 gram
¼ ounce	7 grams
½ ounce	14 grams
1 ounce	28 grams
1¼ ounces	35 grams
1½ ounces	40 grams
1¾ ounces	50 grams
2½ ounces	70 grams
3½ ounces	100 grams
4 ounces	112 grams
5 ounces	140 grams
8 ounces	228 grams
8¾ ounces	250 grams
10 ounces	280 grams
15 ounces	425 grams
16 ounces (1 pound)	454 grams

VOLUME

TO CONVERT	TO	MULTIPLY
teaspoons	milliliters	teaspoons by 4.93
tablespoons	milliliters	tablespoons by 14.79
fluid ounces	milliliters	fluid ounces by 29.57
cups	milliliters	cups by 236.59
cups	liters	cups by 0.24
pints	milliliters	pints by 473.18
pints	liters	pints by 0.473
quarts	milliliters	quarts by 946.36
quarts	liters	quarts by 0.946
gallons	liters	gallons by 3.785

US	METRIC
1 teaspoon	5 milliliters
1 tablespoon	15 milliliters
¼ cup	60 milliliters
½ cup	120 milliliters
1 cup	230 milliliters
1¼ cups	300 milliliters
1½ cups	360 milliliters
2 cups	460 milliliters
2½ cups	600 milliliters
3 cups	700 milliliters
4 cups (1 quart)	0.95 liter
4 quarts (1 gallon)	3.8 liters

RESOURCES

The following brands are reliable sources of high-quality whole grains and rice. They can be found in supermarkets and online.

Anson Mills
www.ansonmills.com

Arrowhead Mills
www.arrowheadmills.com

Bluebird Grain Farms
https://bluebirdgrainfarms.com

Bob's Red Mill
www.bobsredmill.com

Grain
www.eatgrain.ca

Grain Place Foods
http://grainplacefoods.com

Hodgson Mills
www.hodgsonmill.com

Jovial Foods
https://jovialfoods.com

Lotus Foods
www.lotusfoods.com

Lundberg Family Farms
www.lundberg.com

Shiloh Farms
www.shilohfarms.com

RECIPES BY TYPE

- Curried Red Lentil & Sweet Potato Dal with Kale & Toasted Coconut, 105
- Easiest Ever White Bean Soup + Sun-Dried Tomato Pesto, 102
- Marinated Bean Salad with Roasted Red Peppers & Cucumbers, 98
- Mujadarra with Caramelized Onions & Walnuts + Garlic Yogurt, 99
- Panfried Falafel with Cucumber, Tomatoes, Olives & Romaine + Tahini Sauce, 94
- Roasted Cauliflower & Squash with Black Beans & Avocado + Creamy Chipotle Sauce, 106
- Southwestern Pinto Beans with Swiss Chard & Avocado + Roasted Red Pepper Cashew Sauce, 108

CHICKEN, TURKEY & PORK

- Asian Meatballs with Sesame Broccoli + Sweet & Spicy Glaze, 112
- Chicken, Napa Cabbage & Snow Peas + Coconut Peanut Sauce, 119
- Chicken Burrito Bowls + Guacamole, 115
- Chicken Sausages with Broccoli Rabe & Burrata + Sun-Dried Tomato Pesto, 117
- Crunchy Vietnamese-Inspired Chicken & Rice Salad + Spicy Lime Dressing, 123
- Deconstructed (and Lightened-Up) Pork Banh Mi Bowls + Sriracha Maple Yogurt, 126

- Pork Tenderloin with Warm Red Cabbage & Apple Salad + Apple Cider Pan Sauce, 128
- Sausage Meatballs with Fresh Ricotta & Crispy Broccoli + Quick & Easy Marinara Sauce, 120
- Thai-Inspired Turkey Fried Rice, 124
- Za'atar Chicken with Roasted Cauliflower & Pomegranate Molasses, 125

BEEF & LAMB

- Asian Lettuce Wraps, 133
- Bibimbap-Style Steak with Bok Choy, Carrots & Kimchi + Gochujang Sauce, 137
- Chipotle Marinated Hangar Steak + Avocado, Corn & Tomato Relish, 134
- Grilled Skirt Steak with Sweet Corn & Cabbage Slaw + Roasted Red Pepper Cashew Sauce, 141
- Lamb Kofte with Shaved Carrot Salad + Garlic Yogurt, 144
- Lightened-Up Chili Bowls, 139
- Mojo-Marinated Steak with Grilled Vegetables & Arugula + Mojo Dressing, 142
- Moroccan-Spiced Lamb Patties with Roasted Zucchini + Mint & Cilantro Sauce, 146
- Pan-Seared Steak with Roasted Vegetables + Salsa Verde, 150
- Yogurt-Marinated Lamb Kebabs with Tomato, Cucumber & Feta Salad, 149

SEAFOOD

- Broiled Sea Bass & Eggplant + Maple Miso Glaze, 162
- Crispy Fish Tacos Bowls with Quick Red Cabbage & Lime Slaw + Creamy Chipotle Sauce, 154
- Curry-Roasted Salmon with Tomato-Braised Chickpeas + Minty Yogurt, 158
- Poke Bowls, 164
- Roasted Salmon & Asparagus + Herbed Yogurt Sauce, 157
- Roasted Shrimp with Snow Peas & Sweet Corn + Cilantro Mint Sauce, 155
- Roasted White Fish & Caramelized Carrots + Pistachio Yogurt Sauce, 166
- Slow-Roasted Cod + Tomato & Black Olive Salsa, 170
- Spicy Coconut Shrimp with Kale & Cilantro, 171
- Steamed Mussels with Fennel, White Wine & Tomatoes, 161
- Tuna Niçoise Bowls + Herby Vinaigrette, 169

INDEX

Page numbers in *italic* indicate photos.

KEEP YOUR

CREATIVITY COOKING

WITH MORE

BOOKS FROM STOREY

Join the conversation.
Share your experience with this book, learn more about Storey Publishing's authors, and read original essays and book excerpts at storey.com. Look for our books wherever quality books are sold or call 800-441-5700.

BY LAUREN K. STEIN

Capture the playful side of cooking with charming, full-page illustrations for 75 veggie-centric recipes. From pineapple cilantro salsa and asparagus apple salad to a kale egg scramble, these easy recipes celebrate the unbeatable flavors of fresh ingredients.

BY OLWEN WOODIER

Liven up your cooking with an array of simple pestos, pastes, and purées that use just a few fresh ingredients and showcase flavors from around the globe. An additional 75 recipes encourage you to incorporate pestos into every meal.

BY ELISABETH BAILEY

Transform your weeknight dinners with these 62 make-ahead, freezer-friendly sauces. Flavor-packed classics like All-American Barbecue and Sausage Ragu join creative combinations such as Chorizo Garlic, Pumpkin Coconut Cream, and Gorgonzola-Chive Butter to ensure there's something for every taste.

BY MAGGIE STUCKEY

Bring the neighborhood together with your own soup night, choosing from 90 crowd-pleasing recipes for hearty chowders, chilis, and vegetable soups for any time of year. Additional recipes for salads, breads, and dessert round out the soup night experience.